PRAISE FOR *THANK,*

In *Thank, Praise, Serve, and Obey*, Rev. Weedon plucks ~~the~~ ~~~,
from the grungy bathwater of pietism. This rescue is needed. Godly habits are for godly people. Weedon doesn't explain these habits in general terms, but he encourages them in very specific ways, with helpful, concrete teaching and care. The instruction is not designed to help us win a "good person" award (worthless!), but rather to place us nearer to our Lord Jesus (priceless!).

—Deaconess Rosie Adle
Assistant Director of Deaconess Formation,
Concordia Theological Seminary, Fort Wayne, IN,
Co-author of *LadyLike: Living Biblically*

As a former pietist of thirty-four years, I must confess that I was a bit timid to open the pages of Rev. Weedon's new book, *Thank, Praise, Serve, and Obey*. Was this just another book pointing individuals inward, toward a preoccupation with narcissistic piety? The answer: Absolutely not! In fact, Weedon's book does the exact opposite. Avoiding the pitfalls of an internally focused pietism while at the same time prizing godly virtue, Weedon lays forth a piety that directs the reader outside of himself—toward God and His promises. Using the Small Catechism extensively, Weedon shows how the pious life is not within oneself, but instead is outward, lived in Christ through faith and for one's neighbor through love. Oh, how I wish I could have been given a book like this years ago!

—Rev. Dr. Matthew Richard
Pastor of Zion Lutheran Church, Gwinner, ND,
Author of *Will the Real Jesus Please Stand Up? 12 False Christs*

Personal piety needs ordering no less than the pantry or garage. The holy habits Rev. Weedon describes are given life by his own familiarity with the little ways of a Christian. No question is too simple to escape his anticipation and kind teaching. If family is the school for character, *Thank, Praise, Serve, and Obey* is an invaluable handbook for the family of God.

—Rebekah Curtis
Co-author of *LadyLike: Living Biblically*

Be prepared to see the catechism in a whole new light as Rev. Weedon examines eight godly habits of piety. Far from a self-help book or a to-do checklist, this is a faithful exhortation for Christians to live their calling as children of the King. It is written for all Christians, even—perhaps especially—for those who believe they are already pious enough. Weedon skillfully draws the reader into a deeper understanding of and appreciation for the catechism and the gifts God seeks to bestow on us there as we, in response, learn to "thank, praise, serve, and obey" Him.

—Ruth Meyer
Author of *Our Faith from A to Z* and *Grace Alone*

"Dude, you HAVE to read this book! I mean, it will blow you away! Check it out!" These words, penned by Rev. Weedon in a chapter on "Confessing Christ," are also most appropriate with regard to *Thank, Praise, Serve, and Obey!* In eight chapters, Weedon outlines eight godly habits to bless the lives of "eighth day," new-creation, baptized Christians. He masterfully helps readers take a renewed look at Luther's Small Catechism and its use as a guide in developing a strong, Christ-centered devotional life. This book is an "Easter egg" gem (also defined in the book!) just waiting to bless its readers!

—Rev. Stephen Starke
Hymnwriter,
Pastor of St. John Evangelical Lutheran Church, Bay City, MI

In this book, which might well be subtitled "The Eight Godly Habits of Pious Christians," Rev. Weedon describes the focus and object of godly habits: the triune God and the giving of His gifts of life and salvation to His people. Weedon unpacks the significance of these godly habits and how they provide what he calls "the joy and freedom of living and growing as [God's] beloved children through Jesus Christ." This timely and practical volume helps twenty-first-century Christians consider the place and practice of joyful piety in their daily lives.

—Kevin Hildebrand
Kantor, Concordia Theological Seminary, Fort Wayne, IN

Thank, Praise, Serve, and Obey

Recover the Joys of Piety

by

WILLIAM CHANCELLOR WEEDON

This little work is dedicated to Lauren and Dean, David and Meaghan, and Rebekah and Andy in gratitude for the great joys you each have been in my life. "Blessed is the man who has his quiver filled with them."

Published by Concordia Publishing House
3558 S. Jefferson Avenue, St. Louis, MO 63118-3968
1-800-325-3040 · www.cph.org

Cover art: Shutterstock.com

Manufactured in the United States of America

Library of Congress Cataloging-in-Publication Data

Names: Weedon, William, author.

Title: Thank, praise, serve and obey : recover the joys of piety / by William C. Weedon.

Description: Saint Louis : Concordia Publishing House, 2017. | Includes bibliographical references and index.

Identifiers: LCCN 2017043615 (print) | LCCN 2017047188 (ebook) | ISBN 9780758658296 | ISBN 9780758658289 (alk. paper)

Subjects: LCSH: Piety. | Spiritual life--Lutheran Church. | Christian life--Lutheran authors.

Classification: LCC BV4647.P5 (ebook) | LCC BV4647.P5 W44 2017 (print) | DDC 248.4/841--dc23

LC record available at https://lccn.loc.gov/2017043615

4   5   6   7   8   9   10   26   25   24   23   22   21

Table of Contents

Introduction

———⟫●⟪———

THIS LIFE, THEREFORE, IS NOT GODLINESS BUT THE
PROCESS OF BECOMING GODLY, NOT HEALTH BUT
GETTING WELL, NOT BEING BUT BECOMING, NOT
REST BUT EXERCISE. WE ARE NOT NOW WHAT WE
SHALL BE, BUT WE ARE ON THE WAY. THE PROCESS IS
NOT YET FINISHED, BUT IT IS ACTIVELY GOING ON.
THIS IS NOT THE GOAL BUT IT IS THE RIGHT ROAD.
AT PRESENT, EVERYTHING DOES NOT GLEAM AND
SPARKLE, BUT EVERYTHING IS BEING CLEANSED.

—Martin Luther, "Defense and Explanation of All the Articles" (AE 32:24)

———⟫●⟪———

This book is about piety, and specifically posits that piety is a good thing. That might seem a tad odd. To Christians of yesteryear it would surely be a no-brainer. They would not "get" how any Christian would think piety could be a problem. Yet in recent years it seems that piety has fallen on hard times! I would argue in some circles it has become acquainted with its evil twin, pietism. The result has been a rejection not only of that imposter (a rejection which is meet, right, and salutary), but of piety itself. At the very least, some seem to harbor a suspicion that there is something problematic about a Christian aiming at a pious life. The assumption seems to be that piety is not something which a Christian either cultivates or aims for; it simply happens or else it is not genuine. I heartily disagree with that.

So what is piety and how may it be distinguished from its popular falsification as pietism? In this book, I will seek to show that piety at its root is simply the cultivation of godly habits, habits which befit the household of God, the family of our heavenly Father. That is, piety grows from Baptism, grounded in the gracious adoption that God bestows on us with water and the name of the blessed Trinity. Piety flows from that adoption.

Think about our earthly adoptions for a moment. A child is legally declared to be a member of a new family. That child, then, is a member of that family objectively; his or her behavior does not have anything to do with obtaining that new status. The parents rejoice and celebrate the gift of the new member of their family. But part of that family is how their lives are ordered together in a certain way. The family has patterns into which the adopted child will now grow. So it is with the household of faith, the family of God. There are habits that mark how the children of the heavenly Father live in this world as they wait for their Lord's return.

You will no doubt notice that these godly habits seem to share an interesting trait: they all fight against the inward focus that your corrosive original sin supplies. They all fight the fatal "bend in on one's self" that is the telltale sign of the corruption of our human nature. I! Me! Mine! I feel! I think! I want! I, I, I! On the contrary, the habits we will explore in this book foster a joyous freedom from this internal obsession. They train our attention outside of being preoccupied with ourselves, toward God and His promises, and toward our neighbor in love and care for her or his needs. Through these habits, the Spirit of the living God puts His finger, as it were, under our chin and gently lifts our head upward and outward, inviting us into wonder and love. "A Christian lives not in himself," wrote Martin Luther. "He lives in Christ through faith, in his neighbor through love" (AE 31:371).

By way of contrast, the hallmark of pietism is its constant inward focus, its never-ending preoccupation with oneself, even if that means one's "spiritual self." It is characterized by the obsession to monitor carefully one's spiritual pulse by devising all kinds of metrics to measure one's spiritual health and by monitoring and managing one's progress in the faith (with the invariable side-glance to how well one is stacking up against one's neighbor!). Pietism lives by its spiritual "to-do lists" and rules. Pietism likes to stand in front of the mirror, flex a spiritual muscle or two, admire its reflection, and then naturally expect others to admire those spiritual abs too! It delights in the "specific, measurable, and attainable" language of our goals-oriented workplaces. Being, therefore, thoroughly grounded in the Law, pietism lands its devotees where the Law always lands people: either in a blind, pharisaical pride in their own achievement or, in their more honest moments, in despair and doubt and fear.

Jesus contrasts the two approaches in John 8:31–36 when He speaks of the very nature of the freedom that He wants to give:

"If you abide in My word, you are truly My disciples, and you will know the truth, and the truth will set you free."

They answered Him, "We are offspring of Abraham and have never been enslaved to anyone. How is it that You say, 'You will become free'?"

Jesus answered them, "Truly, truly, I say to you, everyone who practices sin is a slave to sin. The slave does not remain in the house forever; the son remains forever. So if the Son sets you free, you will be free indeed."

The mark of the slave is that he has no permanent place in the household and thus fear and doubt dominate his existence. Servile fear that the day will come when he or she will be shown to the door! Hence there is constant checking: "Have I done all that the Master requires? Will he be angry with me? Better check and double check. My very continuation here in the safety of this household hangs on it!"

But if the Son sets you free, you will be free indeed. And this is the truth that the Son has brought us: through our Baptism into our Lord Jesus, we have been clothed in Christ and He has made us joint-heirs with Him, children with Him of His Father, members of the household of God. He came forth from His Father a single Son, but He returned to the Father bringing a family of brothers and sisters with Him. Baptized into Jesus, you are no longer a slave but an heir, a beloved child!

In the comfort of that truth, piety is born and learns to breathe deeply the bracing air of freedom. How utterly free is the man or woman who knows that he or she is loved by God with a love that is amazing, vast, and rock solid! In that freedom, the Christian starts to see the dignity that has been bestowed through Baptism into Christ. Because of our Baptism, we can pray with Jesus, "Our Father . . ." In Christ, we are free to have the eager eyes of children watching our "older Brother" and "dear Father" and learning to do what they do, to follow in the patterns they teach us, and thus to allow the habits of godliness to form us and shape us.

Throughout this book, you will no doubt observe an extensive use of Martin Luther's Small Catechism. I am convinced that Luther's little handbook has been grossly misused among us. We have isolated it from life, attempted to extract doctrine from it, and then teach that doctrine as mere information. We have ignored the vital context the book explicitly describes over and over again. The Small Catechism was not written for and was never meant to live in a classroom! Confining it there results in its true genius being ignored, or worse, subverted. The heading of each of the Chief Parts that Luther wrote teach us where the catechism lives: *"As the head of the family should teach it in a simple way to his household."*

We have made, then, quite a serious blunder when we forget that the catechism was not prepared for pastors to indoctrinate young catechumens, but for pastors to teach parents (and particularly fathers) how they can teach and live the Christian faith in their homes; this was an essential part of nourishing the members of God's household through habits of godliness. The Small Catechism is a primer for the household to learn the joys of life together in God's family! In other words, it is first and foremost a book of piety, of training in godly habits. That's why you'll find prayer breaking out all over (even in the middle of the starkest doctrinal explanations): "Help us to do this, dear Father in heaven!" "Protect us from this, heavenly Father!" (First Petition). That's why you'll find in it instructions about standing or kneeling when you pray, about reverently folding hands at the table when you ask grace or return thanks, about signing yourself with the holy cross, and so on. You'll certainly learn doctrine, for every godly habit of true piety is grounded in the truth of God's love for us in Christ Jesus. Yet, the focus of Luther's Chief Parts is to invigorate joy in our adoption as children of the heavenly Father through Christ, as the Spirit trains us to live in the energizing freedom of that adoption.

We'll also make quite a bit of use in this book of Luther's Large Catechism. There, Luther teaches the mystery of not moving beyond but ever deeper into the great truths of the faith, truths which can never be finally or fully exhausted in this life. And of course, the Christian Book of Concord will also be a trusty road map to explore how to properly hear in the Scriptures our heavenly Father summoning us to the joy and freedom of living and growing as His beloved children through Jesus Christ.

It is my prayer that this little book will provide some solid encouragement and direction for the people of God so that they might know "how one ought to behave in the household of God, which is the church of the living God, a pillar and buttress of the truth" (1 Timothy 3:15) as they seek "to live self-controlled, upright, and godly lives in the present age, waiting for the blessed hope, the appearing of the glory of our great God and Savior Jesus Christ, who gave Himself for us to redeem us from all lawlessness and to purify for Himself a people for His own possession who are zealous for good works" (Titus 2:12–14).

William Weedon
The Day of Sts. Philip and James, 2017

CHAPTER 1

THE FIRST GODLY HABIT:
Faithful Listening to the Word of God

OUR LORD SPEAKS AND WE LISTEN. HIS WORD BESTOWS
WHAT IT SAYS. FAITH THAT IS BORN FROM WHAT IS HEARD
ACKNOWLEDGES THE GIFTS RECEIVED WITH EAGER
THANKFULNESS AND PRAISE. MUSIC IS DRAWN INTO THIS
THANKFULNESS AND PRAISE, ENLARGING AND ELEVATING
THE ADORATION OF OUR GRACIOUS GIVER GOD.

—*Lutheran Worship*, Introduction, p. 6

IT STARTS WITH THE WORD

Piety begins with the Word. It begins with God speaking. That should hardly surprise us, for the Scriptures reveal that is exactly how everything began. God spoke, and what He spoke came to be. We learn from the very beginning, then, that what makes His speaking qualitatively different from ours is His speaking creates and bestows what it says.

The Church has always experienced this odd reality with the Sacred Scriptures. There is a power in these writings that is simply not of human origin. It doesn't arise from the writers, who were all fractured and damaged human beings, even though they were inspired by the Holy

1

Spirit. Rather, the power comes from the Author who stands behind the writers, the Author who inspired their words in such a way that while remaining truly their words, they are *His* Word. Nor is the power merely in the Author. The power in these words is above all because of the One we meet in the Author's words. The One who was always there, even in the pages of the Old Testament, at times deeply hidden, but who steps out to meet us in the pages of the New Testament. The Spirit prompted the writing of these Scriptures and carried them along, but the One whom the Spirit never tires of pointing us to is the Son, our Lord Jesus Christ.

Now, we don't try to prove this to those who are outside the faith. That would be a hopeless venture, if there ever was one! Instead, we invite those who don't believe to come and join us as we hear God speak to us from the Scriptures and see for themselves. Only after they taste firsthand that "the LORD is good" will they be persuaded that "blessed is the man who takes refuge in Him" (Psalm 34:8).

You see, the Church's experience and the conviction that has always taken hold of her because of that experience is that her faith comes to her as a gift through the Word that she hears. St. Paul stated this clearly when he wrote to the Romans, "So faith comes from hearing, and hearing through the word of Christ" (Romans 10:17). The "word of Christ" here means above all "the Word about Christ, the Word in which we meet Christ," and that Word is indeed the Sacred Scriptures.

Notice that St. Paul intentionally used the present tense. Faith *comes*. Not that it came once upon a time; but that it comes—and continues to come. Thus, faith is a constant gift that the Holy Spirit delights to give us as we hear the word of Christ. But we cannot possess it any more than we can possess air or food. Faith is something that we have the joy of constantly receiving. Just as it does not arise from

> FAITH IS A CONSTANT GIFT THAT THE HOLY SPIRIT DELIGHTS TO GIVE US AS WE HEAR THE WORD OF CHRIST

within us but comes to us as a gift from outside, through the Word, even so it is not sustained by anything within us; rather it continually comes to us, ever new, from the outside.

The Small Catechism reflects this reality when it expounds upon the Third Article of the Apostles' Creed. There, we learn: "I believe that I cannot by my own reason or strength believe in Jesus Christ, my Lord, or come to Him; but the Holy Spirit has called me by the Gospel, enlightened me with His gifts, sanctified and kept me in the true faith. In the same way He calls, gathers, enlightens, and sanctifies the whole Christian church on earth, and keeps it with Jesus Christ in the one true faith." Again, not that I "could not" believe by my own reason or strength, but that I "cannot" by my own reason or strength believe. The Holy Spirit's calling, gathering, enlightening and sanctifying work must be ongoing in order for faith to continue to exist. And the means by which He calls us, to which He gathers us, and through which He enlightens and thereby sanctifies us is always the Word.

And thus the very first habit of godliness, the foundational habit upon which any piety or godliness clings for its dear life, is attending to God's Word. This Word alone has the power to give and to sustain the gift of faith in our lives. Piety has to start here; and from the habit of attending to this Word, all the other habits of godliness flow in due course.

NOT A ME THING, BUT A WE THING

This attending to the Word is first of all a corporate activity rather than an individual one; it is first a we thing before it becomes a me thing. "For neither you nor I could ever know anything about Christ or believe in Him and receive Him as our Lord if it were not first offered to us and laid on our hearts by the Holy Spirit through the preaching of the Gospel" (F. Samuel Janzow, *Luther's Large Catechism* [St. Louis: Concordia Publishing House, 1978], 73; hereafter, Janzow). That is, "He has a very special community in the world, which is the mother that brings forth and bears every Christian through the Word of God. The Holy Spirit reveals and proclaims that Word; He uses it to shed His light into human hearts and set them aglow; He empowers them to grasp the Word, accept it, cling to it, and faithfully stay with it" (Janzow 73). Here is how it works:

> I believe that a holy little flock or community exists on earth consisting entirely of saints under one head, Christ. It is called together by the Holy Spirit into one faith, one mind, one understanding. It possesses a variety of gifts, yet is united in love without sect or schism. I too am a part, a member of it. I am a copartner, participating and sharing in all its blessings. I was brought to and incorporated in this community by the Holy Spirit through my hearing and my continuing to hear the Word of God, which is the first step for entering the Christian church. . . . Through this community He gathers us; through it He proclaims and applies the Word by which He creates and multiplies sanctification in order that His community may grow in numbers and become strong in faith and in the fruits of faith, which are the Spirit's creation. (Janzow 74–75)

Said most simply, the Holy Spirit's normal way of bringing people to faith is through the Church. He works through the Office of the Ministry in the Church to proclaim that Word and administer the Sacraments (which are other forms of that Word). He brings hearers together to give and strengthen the faith that binds their hearts to the Lord Jesus. Hearing the Word starts in a community whom the Holy Spirit calls together through that Word and gathers around that Word. In that community, the Word is read aloud and preached. The community knows that it is able to continue as a community of faith only because it devotes itself to listening to the Word. The world never ceases to be amazed that Christians can continue to exist, always listening to a book whose last bits were written two thousand years ago. Christians know the reason their community exists at all is precisely because they do exactly that—always listen to God's Word.

The Formula of Concord, the very last of the Lutheran Confessions to be penned, also shines some interesting light on this point in a few places. First, when discussing the freed will, the Formula of Concord reads,

> **It is not God's will that anyone should be damned, but that all people should be converted to Him and be saved eternally [2 Peter 3:9].**

> *Say to them, As I live, declares the Lord GOD,*
> *I have no pleasure in the death of the wicked,*
> *but that the wicked turn from his way and live.*
> *(Ezekiel 33:11)*

> *For God so loved the world, that He gave His*
> *only Son, that whoever believes in Him should*
> *not perish but have eternal life. [John 3:16]*

Out of His immense goodness and mercy, God provides for the public preaching of His divine eternal Law and His wonderful plan for our redemption, that of the holy, only saving Gospel of His eternal Son, our only Savior and Redeemer, Jesus Christ. By this preaching, He gathers an eternal Church for Himself from the human race and works in people's hearts true repentance, knowledge of sins, and true faith in God's Son, Jesus Christ. By this means, and in no other way (i.e., through His holy Word, when people hear it preached or read it, and through the holy Sacraments when they are used according to His Word), God desires to

call people to eternal salvation. He desires to draw them to Himself and convert, regenerate, and sanctify them. (FC SD II:49–50)

The Formula also references this when pondering the great mystery of election:

Furthermore, the declaration in John 6:44 is right and true, "No one can come to Me unless the Father who sent Me draws him." However, the Father will not do this without means, but has ordained His Word and Sacraments for this purpose as ordinary means and instruments. It is not the will of the Father or of the Son that a person should not hear or should despise the preaching of His Word and wait for the drawing of the Father without the Word and Sacraments. For the Father draws indeed by the power of His Holy Spirit. However, He works according to His usual way. He works by the hearing of His holy, divine Word, as with a net [Matthew 13:47–48], by which the elect are plucked from the devil's jaws. Every poor sinner should therefore attend to the Word, hear it attentively, and not doubt the Father's drawing. For the Holy Spirit will be with His Word in His power, and will work by it. That is the Father's drawing. (FC SD XI:76–77)

We may summarize the point thus far with the simple statement: I come to my personal faith through God's Word at work in a special community, the community called the Church. And this community tends to meet on a certain day to gather around the Word together. We must now consider the certain day on which the Church gathers.

FROM SABBATH TO LORD'S DAY

Although the Old Testament regulation about observing the Sabbath Day was fulfilled in Christ and set aside, as Paul explicitly teaches in Colossians 2:16–17, the wisdom that was imbedded in gathering publicly around the Word of God each week shaped the Christian Church's life from the start. This is only natural, as we see the Lord Jesus Himself practicing the godly habit of attending the synagogue on the Sabbath Day:

> And He came to Nazareth, where he had been brought up. And as was His custom, He went to the synagogue on the Sabbath day, and He stood up to read. And the scroll of the prophet Isaiah was given to Him. He unrolled the scroll and found the place where it was written, "The Spirit of the Lord is upon Me, because He has anointed Me to proclaim good news to the poor. He has sent Me to proclaim liberty to the captives and recovering of sight to the blind, to set at liberty those who are oppressed, to proclaim the year of the Lord's favor." And He rolled up the scroll and gave it back to the attendant and sat down. And the eyes of all in the synagogue were fixed on Him. And He began to say to them, "Today this Scripture has been fulfilled in your hearing." (Luke 4:16–21)

Think of the implications of this! The One whose Spirit inspired the holy writings, the One testified to in these writings, He makes it a habit to devote the Sabbath Day to hearing those writings. The day of rest for God's people was above all a day for resting in the words of Moses and the prophets and the Psalms.

Jesus no doubt gathered with His disciples in the synagogue each Sabbath, and by His teaching and preaching and miracles, He showed

Himself to be the fulfillment of the very Scriptures that were read there. It was the most natural thing in the world for the Church to pick up this pattern from the synagogue and continue it. After all, we now *know* whose Word this is, whom the Spirit was writing about and hinting at from the very beginning. True, Christians moved the day away from the Jewish Sabbath and onto the Day of the Resurrection. But a gathering around the Word has marked the people of God in both Testaments. Thus, the writer to the Hebrews could urge: "Therefore, brothers, since we have confidence to enter the holy places by the blood of Jesus, by the new and living way that He opened for us through the curtain, that is, through His flesh, . . . let us draw near with a true heart in full assurance of faith, . . . not neglecting to meet together, as is the habit of some, but encouraging one another, and all the more as you see the Day drawing near" (Hebrews 10:19–22, 25). No, the observance of the Lord's Day is not to be treated as a new Sabbath law; yet from the start, the day was devoted to coming together as the Church to hear the Word read and preached. We see that pattern developing very early on, even among the Christians in the New Testament (for example Acts 20:7; 1 Corinthians 16:2; Revelation 1:10).

By the middle of the second century, a definite shape for this gathering had developed, a shape which has remained the basis for all historic liturgies[1] since, even those practiced in the Church today.

In the middle of the second century, within fifty years of St. John the apostle and evangelist's death, St. Justin Martyr writes in his First Apology about the Christian gathering:

And on the day called Sunday, all who live in cities or in the country gather together to one place, and the memoirs of the apostles or the writings of the prophets are read, as long

---

1. Liturgy is the term for the traditional way that the Word shaped the Christian meeting across many centuries.

as time permits; then, when the reader has ceased, the president verbally instructs, and exhorts to the imitation of these good things. Then we all rise together and pray, and, as we before said, when our prayer is ended, bread and wine and water are brought, and the president in like manner offers prayers and thanksgivings, according to his ability, and the people assent, saying Amen; and there is a distribution to each, and a participation of that over which thanks have been given, and to those who are absent a portion is sent by the deacons. (*First Apology of Justin* 65 [ANF 1:186–7])

Unpack what St. Justin described as happening in the early second century, and you get this: the people of God come together in one place on the day that the Lord Jesus rose from the dead. They gather in order to hear God's Word read to them, preached, prayed, and then sacramentally received in the Eucharist. Underneath the variations in the details of all historic liturgies, these core elements are consistent through all the centuries and up until today, just as it was when St. Justin wrote.

THE LIFE OF CHRIST:
THE PATTERN FOR READING

Over time, a pattern developed of how and when to read various parts of the Word of God, as well as the songs and prayers that accompanied that reading, proclaiming, and interpreting of it. The pattern is what we call the Church Year. Since this is a development by the Church, how she chooses to read the Word, it must not to be construed as something commanded in the Word itself. *That* she proclaims the Word is a command from God; *how* she organizes the way she does so is not. What she reads on the Lord's Day remains in the area of Christian freedom. Yet, the Lutheran Church historically saw great benefit in the way that the Church Year had developed and particularly in how the Church Year allowed the Word of God to do its sanctifying work among the people of God. Lutherans overwhelmingly chose (and choose) freely to retain it.

The key to the Church Year is always the life and teaching of our Lord Jesus. In current practice, we normally read three passages from the Word of God each time we gather for the Divine Service. There is usually a reading from the Old Testament (though it is sometimes replaced in the Easter season by a reading from the Acts of the Apostles or Revelation), a reading from one of the Epistles (letters written by the apostles), and finally a reading from one of the four Gospels. In the Three-Year Lectionary Series, Year A is predominantly given over to Gospel readings from St. Matthew; Year B to readings from St. Mark; Year C to readings from St. Luke. St. John appears during Easter in all three years as well as during Year B, since Mark is the shortest Gospel. The One-Year Lectionary Series, as its name implies, repeats the same readings annually. The progression of Epistle and Gospel readings in the Series originates several hundred years before the time of Martin Luther. The present One-Year Lectionary Series adds Old Testament readings that are closely related to the respective Gospel reading. In the Three-Year and the One-Year Series, it is always the Gospel reading that ties all of the readings on a Sunday together, helping us to hear the entirety of the Scriptures as the Spirit's witness to the Son.

Because of the way the Church Year tracks with the events and teachings of our Lord's life, the person who makes a godly habit of attending the Divine Service each Sunday (as well as special feast and festival days that fall during weekdays[2]) is immersed in the life and words of Christ in such a way that he or she witnesses the astonishing events of Jesus' earthly life every year. We overhear the Angel Gabriel announce His birth to the Virgin Mother. We hear the heavens ringing

---

2. For example, Thanksgiving, Christmas Eve and Day, New Year's Eve and Day, Ash Wednesday, Maundy Thursday, Good Friday, and the Ascension of our Lord.

with angel song and creep in with the shepherds to adore with the Holy Family at the manger. We see the old man in the temple hold the babe and sing of Him as the light

> HE OR SHE WITNESSES THE ASTONISHING EVENTS OF JESUS' EARTHLY LIFE EVERY YEAR.

of the nations and Israel's glory. Standing by Jordan's banks, we see the heavens torn open, the Spirit descend, and the Father proclaim Christ His own beloved Son. We see Jesus hungry and thirsty beyond limit as He battles Satan in the wilderness, conquering him by the Word, refusing the temptation to doubt the goodness and love of the Father, the exact temptation that felled our first parents. We follow Him back to Galilee and watch miracle after miracle and soak in teaching after teaching, the love He manifests leaving us speechless. We follow along to Jerusalem where the long-expected King arrives to loud shouts of hosanna, but before long we see Him crowned with thorns and robed in garments of mockery. We hide our eyes as He is flogged and beaten. Then, we follow along as He climbs Golgotha's slope and is nailed to the tree. We listen as He there pleads for our forgiveness, pouring out His blood, yielding His life, announcing our completed salvation, and giving over His spirit. We creep to the tomb on Easter morning with the women to be surprised by the joy beyond all joys: Christ is risen from the dead, never to die again!

We experience our doubts with Thomas in the Upper Room, but we also hear Jesus' voice speak "Peace!" which puts our fears to flight. We see Him ascend until the cloud hides Him from view and we hear His angels promise that He will return again, just as we have seen Him go. We wait with the disciples for the promised Spirit, and then with them we proclaim in many tongues the great deeds of God. And as we spread the Word of Christ's triumph, we ponder deeply His teachings and wait with hope for His promised final appearing, the triumph of love and light and laughter. And all the while, as we witness and wait, we pray: Come, Lord Jesus!

This is the life of the assembly. Each year, every year is then anno Domini, the Lord's year (that's what AD means). So Christians have marked their journey through time by marking the Life witnessed to in the Gospels, the Life who alone is the key to unlocking the Old Testament and life itself.

Out from our Lord's life the rest of the Scriptures are then received and heard correctly. The result of attending to hearing the Scriptures read publicly is that the Holy Spirit begins to shape the mind of Christ within us. We come to value what Christ values, to love what He loves, to desire what He desires, to see our lives and the lives of others as He sees them. Above all, in Him we come to know and believe the love God has for us and for all the world. And this is how the Word of God sanctifies us. Luther says:

As we have heard, people are made holy only through God's Word. Places, times, persons, and the entire external order of worship have been instituted and appointed in order that God's Word may publicly do this work of making people holy. (Janzow 27)

When Jesus called the disciples, He invited: "Follow Me!" And the Church has ever after taken Him up on the invitation by proclaiming and pondering His conception, birth, life, death, resurrection, and return through her public reading of the Word of God. The entire liturgical structure exists for that reason and that reason alone. You don't "come to church" in order to do something for God. That's completely backwards. He doesn't need a thing you've got or can do; but you need Him. You need His Word. You need it more than you need food or water, light and air. "Man shall not live by bread alone, but by every word that comes from the mouth of God" (Matthew 4:4). Jesus threw that quote from Deuteronomy in the devil's face when the evil one was tempting Him to think that life was all about a full belly, or that the

Father's love depends on that full belly. It's not, and it doesn't. There's so much more. We'll never discover what that "more" entails until we realize that our loving heavenly Father assembles us together first and foremost so that He might do something for us, to impart to us a share in real life, the life that is in His Son. He assembles us to fill us with His joy and His peace and to let us bask in His amazing love. That is, He gathers us together as the Church in order to speak His Word to us; and that Word, alive with the power of the Holy Spirit, changes absolutely everything.

THE SUNDAY PRIVILEGE AND JOY

Because this is so, we can see why the Small Catechism explicates the Third Commandment in this way:

Remember the Sabbath day by keeping it holy.

What does this mean?

**We should fear and love God so that we do
not despise preaching and His Word, but hold
it sacred and gladly hear and learn it.**

To despise does not mean to hate; it means to think little of, to regard something as unimportant and unworthy of your time or consideration. So I break this commandment whenever I find that the public reading and preaching of the Word is not as important as some other options in my life. In case you have not noticed, the world and the devil are more than happy to fill up your calendar with other regularly scheduled activities! Give the devil an inch and he takes a mile. Suspicious how many of these extra activities seem to fall squarely on Sunday, no?

Now, each of these activities in themselves may be a blessing, but they become deadly when they choke out the space where the Word publicly works in our lives. To be perfectly blunt: to hold the Word sacred and to gladly hear it and learn it means at minimum that any Sunday you are physically able, you will be found with your brothers and sisters attending to the Word of God. This is not to fulfill some "holy day of obligation" as our medieval ancestors erroneously imagined; rather, it is to safeguard space for the privilege and joy of the Word of God doing its great work in your life.

Gladly hear. This is an attitude that is caught more than taught. When parents in a household look forward to the day when they can gather with their sisters and brothers in Christ and receive the Word read and preached and the body and blood of their Savior distributed, then the children, too, come to look forward to that day. When the dad or mom groan, "Well, I guess we have to go to church today. Jimmy is supposed to acolyte," Jimmy hears loud and clear that this is not something his parents actually want to do or anticipate doing with joy. Usually, that happens because his parents have never understood that Sunday is all about God coming, in unfathomable grace, to serve up His salvation for them in the Word read, preached, tasted, and sung.

ON LISTENING TO PREACHING

A brief word on preaching is in order. God did not send the preacher to your congregation to make you happy. God really is not ultimately interested in your happiness and neither should you be. He sent the preacher there to make you holy by speaking the Word to you that alone can do that job. And holiness is a thousand times better than happiness. Happiness literally hangs on what is happening in a moment of time. Holiness is sharing in God's own divine life forever; and that is true, indestructible blessedness and joy.

So many times when I hear people complain that a sermon "just didn't feed" them or "speak to" them, I cannot help but think what is running beneath the surface of their comment is that the preacher didn't tell enough cute stories that made them laugh and feel good about themselves and the world. We would all get much more out of the sermons our pastors faithfully labor to deliver if we put a little more effort into preparing our hearts and minds to hear the Word

> GOD DID NOT SEND THE PREACHER TO YOUR CONGREGATION TO MAKE YOU HAPPY . . . HE SENT THE PREACHER THERE TO MAKE YOU HOLY.

preached. For example, on Saturday night, we could take time to read the lessons for the following day in church. They can be found in the *Lutheran Service Book* on pages xiv–xxiii. We could read them over, out loud and prayerfully. We could let the words fill our mouths, the sounds our ears, resounding in our hearts and minds. Is there something in the reading that puzzles or troubles you? Anything there that angers you? Anything that simply confuses you? Something there that challenges or frightens you with the prospect of changing something in your life? Is there anything in the readings that comforts you? Anything that amazes you and leaves you awestruck? As you read the texts and think of these questions, you may even wish to write down your thoughts or, if you are reading them aloud with your family, to talk about them together in anticipation of the Sunday sermon. Do this, and then come to the Sunday sermon and notice how you experience it. I think you would be astonished at the difference this kind of preparation makes in how you hear the preaching of God's Word. This extra time of engagement with the readings will help you to hold preaching and God's Word as sacred in your heart and mind.

One more thing: if your pastor seems to be struggling with preaching on a particular Sunday, why not stop and say a prayer for him right then and there, asking that he might speak God's Word to you and the rest of the congregation with clarity and with joy, so that the Word may not be hindered from doing the work God sends it to do?

ATTENDING CHURCH IS NOT AUTOMATICALLY
ATTENDING TO THE WORD!

"Great," you might be thinking, "so the point is 'go to church.' I got that one down." Now, before you go too far down that path, hear the warning: attending the Sunday service is important and even necessary; but it is not in and of itself sufficient. You see, attending to the Word is not just a matter of hearing it, but of learning it. "Gladly hear *and learn it.*"

We must face the fact that it is entirely possible to attend to the reading and preaching of God's Word faithfully, week in and week out, and still not benefit from it. This is not through any fault of the Word itself, but rather because our own sinfulness stops our ears and distracts our attention. Our Lord's parable of the sower poignantly points this out. Listen to His explanation of the parable:

> *Now the parable is this: The seed is the word of God. The ones along the path are those who have heard. Then the devil comes and takes away the word from their hearts, so that they may not believe and be saved. And the ones on the rock are those who, when they hear the word, receive it with joy. But these have no root; they believe for a while, and in time of testing fall away. And as for what fell among the thorns, they are those who hear, but as they go on their way they are choked by the cares and riches and pleasures of life, and their fruit does not mature. As for that in the good soil, they are those who, hearing the word, hold it fast in an honest and good heart, and bear fruit with patience. (Luke 8:11–15)*

Note that apart from the Word, faith cannot exist. And note that the Word can be satanically stolen away because of inattention, lost by letting go of it in times of suffering, or choked out of our lives by worries or concerns for money and pleasure. In every case, the loss of the Word is the loss of faith, and significantly, in the parable it happens in those who do in fact "hear." Jesus is not addressing the hordes of those who disregard Him; He is dealing (as He so often does) with those who are actually listening to Him (see also Matthew 7:24–27, "Everyone then who hears these words of Mine . . .").

In the Large Catechism, Luther ponders this sad possibility of hearing and yet not keeping the Word as he leads us to meditate on the Third Commandment:

> Those who grossly misuse and desecrate the holy day, those, for example, who neglect God's Word because of greed or frivolity or who laze about in taprooms, drinking and stuffing themselves like swine, are not the only ones who violate this commandment. It is transgressed also by that other crowd who listen to God's Word as to some entertainment and come to the preaching service merely by the force of habit and leave again with as little understanding of the Word at the end of the year as at the beginning. . . . Today we do have God's Word, but we nevertheless fail to eliminate its misuse; we let ourselves be preached to and admonished, but we listen without earnestness and serious concern. (Janzow 28)

Luther contrasts this lighthearted approach to the Word with what happens when one forms the godly habit of not merely attending the Divine Service, but of actually *paying attention* to the Word read and preached—actually learning it:

> On the other hand, when we sincerely ponder, hear, and apply the Word, it has such power that its fruit never fails.

The Word always awakens new understandings, new delights, and a new spirit of devotion, and it constantly cleanses our heart and our thinking. For here are not limp and lifeless words, but words that are alive and move to living action. (Janzow 28–29)

We can see, then, that we are not speaking of the power of the Word in some magical sense. Just putting yourself where its sounds will float in one ear and out the other accomplishes exactly nothing. Rather, think of what the Blessed Virgin Mary did when she was confronted with great words of God, words that sometimes she could not fully comprehend. "But Mary treasured up all these things, pondering them in her heart" (Luke 2:19). "And they did not understand the saying that He spoke to them. . . . And His mother treasured up all these things in her heart" (Luke 2:50–51).

"Treasuring up" and "pondering in the heart" is what I mean by attending to the Word. Psalm 1 describes this attention like this:

> Blessed is the man who walks not in the counsel of the wicked, nor stands in the way of sinners, nor sits in the seat of scoffers; but his delight is in the law of the LORD, and on His law he meditates day and night. (Psalm 1:1–2)

Delight! This is not some grim "have to" but a joyous "get to"! Some have suggested that the concept of "meditate" here is at root connected to eating: a slow chew that extracts every bit of the delicious juice and nourishment from the Word you are "chewing" on.

Or to shift the image, remember Jacob wrestling with the Lord on the banks of the Jabbok in Genesis 32? "I will not let You go unless You bless me." When Jacob realized he had spent the night wrestling with the pre-incarnate Christ, he "called the name of the place Peniel, saying, 'For I have seen God face to face, and yet my life has been delivered'" (Genesis 32:30). Just so does the Lord want us to grab hold of Him in His Word and wrestle until the light dawns. This passage shows it is not disrespectful or impertinent to do so, but rather that our Savior is so gracious He truly does desire us to wrestle with Him in His Word and in prayer.

THE SUNDAY FAMILY MEAL

In the natural rhythm of our family life, people spend most of their days at home or at work, but then there are special occasions when the smaller family unit gathers with the larger family. In years gone by, when folks tended to live fairly close to relatives, Sundays would often be the time the larger family gathered at the grandparents' home. Aunt and uncles, cousins, nieces and nephews, brothers and sisters would all sit down to a large meal together. This weekly gathering was a treasured part of many people's growing up experience in years gone by.

Something like this happens in the Church each Lord's Day. The members of the extended family that form the congregation come together, as many as can possibly be there. And if someone's not there, they are missed, for God has given us this gift of the local congregation as the place where we get to know our brothers and sisters in the faith who love us and help us to live as God's children in this world.

When we gather, we do two things that would be quite familiar to the old-fashioned Sunday dinner with the whole crew assembled! We tell and listen to the family stories and we share together in a meal. That is what the Divine Service really is at its core. Realizing that allows us, then, to understand how important that weekly get-together

> JUST AS A LOVING EARTHLY PARENT WANTS ALL THE CHILDREN AND GRANDKIDS TO BE GATHERED, SO THE HEAVENLY FATHER OUT OF LOVE FOR EACH OF US WANTS US TO BE GATHERED WITH THE REST OF OUR FAMILY, THE CHURCH.

is with the family of our congregation. Just as a loving earthly parent wants all the children and grandkids to be gathered, so the heavenly Father out of love for each of us wants us to be gathered with the rest of our family, the Church. He has gifts He has long prepared for us, and He wants to tell us about them, serve them to us, and fill our hearts with joy and sheer delight.

GIFTS ABOUNDING MORE THAN ONE DAY A WEEK

So, if the first and foundational godly habit is to make space in your life for the Word of God to do its great work within you, does that mean the Third Commandment has exhausted its joys only with reference to Sundays? Said another way, does this mean that the work the Word of God does in the public assembly is the whole of its job? By no means!

There is simply no way that you could fit the great riches contained in the Word of God all into the round of Sundays and feast and festival days, even if you observed them all. Listen to Luther again:

> **Indeed, we Christians ought to observe an ongoing holy day and be totally involved with holy things, that is, daily occupy ourselves with God's Word, carrying it in our hearts and on our lips. (Janzow 26)**

While he recognizes that Christians will always struggle to find ways to do this, Luther still teaches us that the Word is a gift from our loving heavenly Father we can enjoy each and every day. Just as Christians since the time of the New Testament have observed the Lord's Day, they have also allowed the Word to do its work in their homes by giving some portion of the day to reading, hearing, and pondering the Word, and to prayer (which we will discuss in more detail in the next chapter).

Because it can be a struggle to find space in your life for the Word each day, the Church produces numerous helps for a daily time in the Bible that are worth exploring. There are many good ones, but I will mention just three.

The simplest are little devotionals like *Portals of Prayer* which give you a small portion of the Scriptures to chew on each day; these portions usually take less than five minutes to read. I think the greatest value of this kind of devotional is highlighting a verse or two that you can readily think about all day long.

For those of you who want to go a little deeper in your devotions, there is also the comprehensive resource *Treasury of Daily Prayer* (or its app version: *PrayNow*). Here, much wider swaths of the Word are explored than is possible in the Sunday service. The *Treasury* follows *Lutheran Service Book*'s daily lectionary (pp. 299–304), providing the full text of the readings—one from the Old Testament and one from the New Testament. Each day there are also psalms, hymns, prayers, and writings from the Church's inheritance of hearing and thinking about the Word of God over thousands of years. While the *Treasury* doesn't attempt to read the whole Bible in a year, it does expose the user to a good chunk of the Scriptures each day while also following the Church's ancient rhythms of reading certain books of the Bible during certain seasons of the Church Year. The *Treasury* is very easy to follow and simple to use; and it takes about fifteen to twenty minutes a day to complete if you read it out loud.

If you will pardon a personal word, my wife and I generally begin every day at the kitchen table with our own copies of *Treasury* opened, our coffee sitting close at hand. Over the years we, like many others, struggled to establish the godly habit of letting the Word sanctify our home each day. We experimented with various devotional resources, but all with limited success. When the *Treasury* came along, however, everything changed. The struggle was at an end. In its pages we discovered a veritable gold mine that we doubt we will ever be able to exhaust. Using it is simplicity itself. When either of us is on the road, then the mobile version, *PrayNow*, is our go-to.

Whether it comes from using *Treasury of Daily Prayer*, *Portals of Prayer*, or any of many other devotional resources (our Lutheran publishing house, Concordia Publishing House, has many!), finding time in the home for the Word of God to keep doing its great sanctifying work in our lives is an important part of the godly habit of attending to the Word. It also only serves to strengthen our experience in the Divine Service on Sundays and Bible studies we might attend during the week.

One other way: do you have a commute to work? Consider spending some of your time during the year listening to the Bible read to you. You will be amazed at the things you learn and shocked at how much you might have missed in the past. I personally use Audible and usually devote Lent to listening to the Scriptures from start to finish. You'll be shocked at the things you never heard before that will jump out at you.

In all of these ways, we can do what St. Paul exhorts and "let the Word of Christ dwell in you richly." It is, after all, the foundational habit of godliness.

Sing:

> Father, Son, and Spirit, Lord,
> Praise to You and adoration!
> Grant that we may trust Your Word,
> Confident of our salvation,
> While we here below must wander,
> Till we sing Your praises yonder.
>
> —*LSB* 904:4

For Discussion

Scarlet Thread

1. Why is attending to the Word regarded as the foundation of all piety?

   work of godly habits

2. What do we learn about Jesus' observance of this godly habit in Luke 4? *pg 7.*

3. Why did the Church Year develop and how does it help us live in the Word?

   pg 9 bottom
   p10 top + middle
   focus

4. Why would you make hearing the Word on Sundays a priority in your life?

   Word is sacred
   hear + learn it
   be together

5. How is it possible to be a regular attender on Sundays and yet not benefit?

   sinfulness stops our ears, distracts our attention

6. What resources have you found useful for reading the Word in the home?

   Portals of Prayer
   psalms
   hymns
   prayers
   Treasury of daily prayers
   Audible Bible

CHAPTER 2

THE SECOND GODLY HABIT:
The Daily Prayers

When the Small Catechism is removed from its native home, the household, and confined to a classroom, one of the first casualties is the entire second section, labelled "Daily Prayers." The sad result of this has been that many, many Lutheran Christians struggle with prayer. I remember how shocking (but refreshing) it was to hear a devout member of my congregation who almost never missed a Sunday service or Bible class, when asked to serve as sponsor for a new Christian, sheepishly confess: "But I can't teach *him* how to pray, because *I* don't actually know how to pray."

He was certainly not alone. I have heard the lament from more than one person born and raised in the Lutheran Church, "I am not comfortable praying; I am not sure how to do it." And it doesn't help that right away some folks chime in, "That's what you all get for using all those prayer books and liturgies with everything written down. You need to learn to pray from what is in your heart." I think the use of written prayers and prayers handed down through the ages is actually not at all the source of the problem. In

> "I AM NOT COMFORTABLE PRAYING; I AM NOT SURE HOW TO DO IT."

my experience, regularly using the prayers that the Church has handed down to us actually helps enormously when the occasion arises in which one needs or wishes to pray "from the heart."

But not knowing how to pray can be very painful. The Christian feels inadequate and ashamed and terrified that someone may put them on the spot by asking them to pray in public. We know that we are to "pray without ceasing" (1 Thessalonians 5:17) and that we "ought always to pray and not lose heart" (Luke 18:1), but like the person who has gotten by for years by faking literacy, we keep pretending this is not a problem, too ashamed to admit: "We just don't know how to do it!"

Both the Small Catechism and the Large Catechism, however, are replete with solid help for addressing this inadequacy we have neglected so long to our own detriment. We will spend this chapter unpacking those helps.

THE ALTAR OF THE BEDSIDE

HOW THE HEAD OF THE FAMILY SHOULD TEACH HIS HOUSEHOLD TO PRAY MORNING AND EVENING.

—The Small Catechism, p. 32

Granted, the Christian is to pray at all times, but here is a truth: the one who does not learn to pray habitually at set times does not tend to make progress in the art of praying at all times. From the earliest days, the people of God have recognized two times when it is especially appropriate to pray: morning and evening. That is, when you first rise in the morning and before you lie down in your bed to sleep at night. Why these times in particular?

Note that they are both the boundaries of sleep. At no time is a human being so utterly vulnerable as when he or she is sleeping. The psalmist marvels:

"I lay down and slept; I woke again, for the LORD sustained me. I will not be afraid of many thousands of people who have set themselves against me all around." (Psalm 3:5–6)

"In peace I will both lie down and sleep; for You alone, O LORD, make me dwell in safety." (Psalm 4:8)

"O LORD, in the morning You hear my voice; in the morning I prepare a sacrifice for You and watch." (Psalm 5:3)

"You make the going out of the morning and the evening to shout for joy." (Psalm 65:8)

"O LORD, God of my salvation; I cry out day and night before You. Let my prayer come before You; incline Your ear to my cry!" (Psalm 88:1–2)

"It is good to give thanks to the LORD, to sing praises to Your name, O Most High; to declare Your steadfast love in the morning, and Your faithfulness by night." (Psalm 92:1–2)

I could, of course, multiply the examples. The Book of Psalms, the prayer book of the Old Testament, invites us into this rhythm of consciously remembering God and His mercies as both the first and the last act of the day. If prayer is ever to grow like a flourishing vine and then spread out to fill all of our day, it must have a starting place, a place where it is rooted. The catechism teaches us that the starting place is simply when we get up and right before we lie down, two activities that mark human life every day.

Morning Prayer

*In the morning when you get up, make the sign
of the holy cross and say:*

**In the name of the Father and of the ✠
Son and of the Holy Spirit. Amen.**

The German of the Small Catechism reads slightly differently and
might best be rendered:

The power of God, Father, ✠ Son, and Holy Spirit. Amen.

If we ponder this first lesson in prayer, we notice that it involves
our bodies. The prayer that is spoken with our mouth is signaled by
standing. We have received a great mercy from the triune God. He has
kept us in safety through the hours of darkness, when we lay still and
defenseless. And being able to stand up after that time of sleep is already
a grace, an undeserved gift. Just as we neither sought nor asked for life
to be given to us, but it came as a free gift of God's bountiful love, so
the continuation of our lives is not something we take credit for (at
least not if we are being honest). It is the same unexpected, unasked
for gift being extended through all the days of our lives.

But there is more. Sleep is a constant reminder to us of death. It is
not an accident that our Lord Jesus speaks of death as sleep (more on
this in chapter 8!). Think of what Jesus says of Jairus's daughter: "The
child is not dead but sleeping" (Mark 5:39). Think of what Jesus says of
Lazarus: "Our friend Lazarus has fallen asleep, but I go to awaken him"
(John 11:11). If death is but a sleep, then the converse is true: sleep is
a picture of our death, and that means that each morning constitutes
a "resurrection" of sorts. Each morning that we stand up is practice for
the day when the Sun of Righteousness will rise with healing in His
wings and summon the dead to awake: "Do not marvel at this, for an

hour is coming when all who are in the tombs will hear His voice and come out" (John 5:28–29).

Do you see then why our prayer begins with the Invocation of the triune name? The very words by which we were baptized into Christ, by which we were buried with Him in His tomb, and raised with Him

> IF DEATH IS BUT A SLEEP, THEN THE CONVERSE IS TRUE: SLEEP IS A PICTURE OF OUR DEATH, AND THAT MEANS THAT EACH MORNING CONSTITUTES A "RESURRECTION" OF SORTS

into His new life, these are the words that begin each day for us. To make it your habit to stand up in the morning and open your mouth, proclaiming, "In the name of the Father and of the ✠ Son and of the Holy Spirit. Amen" is tantamount to shouting out to all creation, "I am baptized! I have been raised with Christ! My sins are buried in His tomb. I am a child of the resurrection!"

The instruction to make the sign of the holy cross deserves some consideration. There was a time not long ago when Lutherans were afraid to make the sign of the holy cross because someone told them it was a Roman Catholic practice. But although Roman Catholics do indeed use the sign of the holy cross, they most certainly do not own it. Christians of the Orthodox East, Anglicans, and many others freely make this bodily sign. Our catechism instructs parents to teach children to use it! It is usually done by touching the fingertips of the right hand to the forehead, to the navel, and then to the right shoulder and finally to the left, ending up above the heart (some Christians do the final move in reverse, ending up on the right shoulder).

What does the sign of the holy cross suggest? Ownership! It is a way of confessing to whom you belong. "You are not your own, for you were bought with a price," St. Paul reminded the Corinthian Christians (1 Corinthians 6:19–20). That price is the life of the Crucified. He thought you were worth that! Or as St. Paul wrote to the Galatians, "I have been crucified with Christ. It is no longer I who live, but Christ who lives in me. And the life I now live in the flesh I live by faith in the Son of God, who loved me and gave Himself for me" (Galatians 2:19–20). The sign of the cross is also a reminder of Baptism, as the baptismal liturgy (*LSB*, p. 268) says:

The pastor makes the sign of the holy cross upon the forehead and heart of each candidate while saying:

Name, receive the sign of the holy cross both upon your ✠ forehead and upon your ✠ heart to mark you as one redeemed by Christ the crucified.

Rising from the "death" of sleep each day, you mark yourself with this same sign, invoking the triune name: I am not my own. I have been bought. I have been brought into the family of God and I am named as His very own.

As Luther moves forward with the Morning Prayer, he writes,

Then, kneeling or standing, repeat the Creed and the Lord's Prayer.

We note, again, the instructions for the body. Having arisen for the Invocation, we may fall down upon our knees, or alternatively, we may continue standing. What is the import of these actions? Either action is a reminder that we begin this new day in the presence of our Maker, Redeemer, and Sanctifier. If we kneel, the words of Psalm 95 ring out: "Oh come, let us worship and bow down; let us kneel before the LORD, our Maker!" (Psalm 95:6) If we stand, we remember Nehemiah 9:5, "Stand up and bless the LORD your God from everlasting to everlasting. Blessed be Your glorious name, which is exalted above all blessing and praise." Both are postures of prayer to Him in whose presence we find ourselves.

His presence is very much tied to His name. We think not only of how Aaron was instructed to put the name of God upon the people so that the Lord would bless them (see Numbers 6), but also of how the name of God had a place, a dwelling, in the temple. Solomon prayed,

"Yet have regard to the prayer of Your servant and to his plea, O LORD my God, listening to the cry and to the prayer that Your servant prays before You this day, that Your eyes may be open night and day toward this house, the place of which You have said, 'My name shall be there,' that You may listen to the prayer that Your servant offers toward this place. And listen to the plea of Your servant and of Your people Israel, when they pray toward this place. And listen in heaven Your dwelling place, and when You hear, forgive" (*1 Kings 8:28–30*).

Where God has placed His name, He has placed Himself. And His name was placed on your body on the very day you were baptized "into" the name of the Father and of the Son and of the Holy Spirit! So now you begin each day with the recognition that your body has become God's temple. "Or do you not know that your body is a temple of the Holy Spirit within you, whom you have from God? You are not your own, for you were bought with a price. So glorify God in your body" (1 Corinthians 6:19–20).

The next item sounds strange to our ears. Why is the Creed included in morning prayers? Isn't it rather just a statement of belief? It is a statement of belief, of course. (The word *creed* comes from the Latin *credo*, "I believe.") But when we speak it in the presence of the God who has made us His own children in Baptism and has made our bodies into His temple, then it is our prayer as well. We simply are saying back to Him in summary what He has said to us; and our very confession of

31

what He has said to us is a plea that He keep us in this faith—since it is not of our invention but of His revealing.

The Creed Luther intends here is the Apostles' Creed. At the start of each day, then, we recite—kneeling or standing in God's presence—this summary of the Church's faith as our own faith. In the Large Catechism, Luther says:

> For in these three articles God Himself has revealed and disclosed the deepest profundity of His fatherly heart, His sheer inexpressible love. He created us for the very purpose that He might redeem us and make us holy. And besides giving and entrusting to us everything in heaven and on earth, He has given us His Son and His Holy Spirit in order to bring us to Himself through them. For, as we explained earlier, we were totally unable to come to a recognition of the Father's favor and grace except through the Lord Christ, who is the mirroring image of the Father's heart. Without Christ we see nothing in God but an angry and terrible Judge. But we could know nothing of Christ either, if it were not revealed to us by the Holy Spirit. (Janzow 77)

This is to say that the praying of the Creed reminds us exactly to whom we are praying and what this triune God has done, still does, and will continue to do for us.

After the Creed, we turn to the Lord's Prayer. We will discuss this prayer in detail later in the chapter, but at this point we will mention that this is the prayer that our Lord Jesus Himself gave His disciples when they begged Him to teach them how to pray. He introduced it to them with the instruction, "When you pray, say . . ." (Luke 11:2). The Church has always taught this prayer from Jesus as the perfect Christian prayer, indeed the very rule of all prayer and the inexhaustible treasury of prayer. The more a Christian uses this prayer, the more one realizes that it enfolds in its brief words absolutely every request we will ever need to make to our heavenly Father. Yes, it may be expanded (as we do, for example, in Divine Service, Setting Five of the *Lutheran Service Book*, where the Lord's Prayer serves as the Prayer of the Church [see pp. 215–16]). But by far, it is most commonly prayed exactly as Jesus gave it, with the addition of a doxology at the end: "for thine is the kingdom . . ." This the catechism teaches us to do at the dawn of each day.

The opening words of the Lord's Prayer remind us again of the connection with morning and resurrection. Was it not on the first Easter morn after the Lord Jesus had risen from the dead (and made His bed—don't miss that detail in John 20:7!) that He commissioned Mary Magdalene, "Go to My brothers and say to them, 'I am ascending to My Father and *your* Father, to My God and *your* God'" (John 20:17, emphasis added)? Baptized into Christ, we rise each morning and remember that we are truly His brothers and sisters and that, in Him, we may be bold to approach our kind heavenly Father. In Him, we may boldly ask as dear children ask their dear Father!

The catechism goes on:

If you choose, you may also say this little prayer:

I thank You, my heavenly Father, through Jesus Christ, Your dear Son, that You have kept me this night from all harm and danger; and I pray that You would keep me this day also from sin and every evil, that all my doings and life may please You. For into Your hands I commend myself, my body and soul, and all things. Let Your holy angel be with me, that the evil foe may have no power over me. Amen.

In this classic little prayer, Luther has adapted some of the prayers he learned as a monk from the breviary (the monks' massive prayer book) into language that a child can learn and treasure and an adult can never outgrow. Since thanksgiving is always our first duty, the prayer starts by thanking God. We are still alive, having been brought safely through the night. This is not our accomplishment, but a gracious gift from Him who has become our heavenly Father through His Son. We give thanks for safekeeping through the night, but we also know that the day stretches before us, and each day may be beset with perils of its own. So we ask our Father to keep us this day, too, from sin and every evil, that is to prevent sin and evil from conquering us and stealing us away from Him. Rather, we beg that all that we do and the way we live may be pleasing to the Father. This is a daily dose of "not my will, but Yours, be done." In order that this might be so, we place ourselves, body and soul, and all that we hold dear into the Father's loving hands. We beg from Him the companionship of His holy angel to walk with us through the day, so that the evil foe, the wicked one, may not have any power over us.

Though I have expounded the morning prayers in some detail, remember that all of this takes less than two minutes at the start of the day! But making a habit of giving these two minutes to prayer bears huge fruit. In our day, mindfulness is a popular concept. In a sense, mindfulness is what these prayers do for the Christian: they make you mindful of *whose* you are, of how precious you are to Him, and of how pleased He is by faith and the good works that follow.

And that leads to the final instruction of the morning prayers:

Then go joyfully to your work, singing a hymn, like that of the Ten Commandments, or whatever your devotion may suggest.

The morning prayers end with you going off with joy to the work of the day. I do not think it was an accident that among all the hymns that could be sung, Luther singled out the Ten Commandments hymn as appropriate for starting one's work. You can find it in *Lutheran Service Book*, hymn 581, "These Are the Holy Ten Commands." With this hymn, the Christian then will have reviewed the three principal parts of the Small Catechism at the very start of the day: the Ten Commandments, the Creed, and the Lord's Prayer. That is, what God would have us do; what God has done for us; and how to seek His help and aid. The Ten Commandments, after all, are not exhausted in simply showing us that we are sinners. They swing back around at the end of our prayers as veritable gifts, teaching us concrete ways to be a blessing to our neighbor and to live a godly life (more on that in chapter 7).

Evening Prayer

As at the start of your day, so at the end, before you lay your head to rest in a sleep that is always an image and reminder of death, you stop to pray. Prayer is perhaps even harder now than in the morning. You are likely weary, and the bed is so inviting. Yet, we know that sleep, too, is a gift we seek from God. "It is in vain that you rise up early and go late to rest, eating the bread of anxious toil; for He gives to His beloved sleep" (Psalm 127:2)

> THE DAY WILL COME WHEN YOU WILL LIE DOWN IN A BED AND NOT GET UP AGAIN UNTIL RESURRECTION MORNING.

Standing by your bed, then, you end the day as you began it, making the sign of the holy cross and saying:

In the name of the Father and of the ✠ Son and of the Holy Spirit. Amen.

That is, you end the day remembering that you have been baptized. You belong to Christ. You have a Savior. The day will come when you will lie down in a bed and not get up again until Resurrection morning. Each evening is a little rehearsal for that last lying down, a practice for it.

Then, kneeling or standing, repeat the Creed and the Lord's Prayer.

Just as you knelt or stood in God's presence at the start of the day, so you kneel or stand at the close of the day, remembering that you are still in His presence, remembering that "even the darkness is not dark to You; the night is bright as the day, for darkness is as light with You" (Psalm 139:12). You may sleep, but He does not.

> *"My help comes from the* LORD, *who made heaven and earth. He will not let your foot be moved; He who keeps you will not slumber. Behold, He who keeps Israel will neither slumber nor sleep. The* LORD *is your keeper; the* LORD *is your shade on your right hand. The sun shall not strike you by day, nor the moon by night. The* LORD *will keep you from all evil; He will keep your life. The* LORD *will keep your going out and your coming in from this time forth and forevermore"* (Psalm 121:2–8).

Those last words are prayed in the baptismal liturgy as the movement is made toward the font. All of life is lived from the standpoint of our Baptism. It is the start and ending of our day, that event that began our life in Christ and will, on the day of our death, complete it.

I think in the evening the particular part of the Creed that is helpful to focus on is "the forgiveness of sins, the resurrection of the body, and the life everlasting" in the Third Article. Whether this evening is our last on earth or whether there will be many more evenings yet for us, we go to our bed asserting: we will rise, a forgiven people, to a life that never ends!

And perhaps in the evening, the words of forgiveness also in the Lord's Prayer ring most profoundly. For as we reflect upon the doings of the day, we see our many failures to have lived in our baptismal freedom. We recall the moments we slipped back into the old ways and allowed the sinful self to gain an upper hand. Our prayer to be delivered from evil, then, encompasses being delivered from the consequences of the evils we have done that day, foolishly betraying the new life we have in Christ. We take a moment to think back over the day as we pray; and we realize how deeply we need to pray this perfect prayer at the close of this day and of every day: "And forgive us our trespasses as we forgive those who trespass against us." The theme of forgiveness also appears in the Evening Prayer:

> *If you choose, you may also say this little prayer:*

> **I thank You, my heavenly Father, through Jesus Christ, Your dear Son, that You have graciously kept me this day; and I pray that You would forgive me all my sins where I have done wrong, and graciously keep me this night. For into Your hands I commend myself, my body and soul, and all things. Let Your holy angel be with me, that the evil foe may have no power over me. Amen.**

As in the morning, so in the evening, and at all times in between, our first duty is thanksgiving for the gifts God has showered upon us unceasingly. The Evening Prayer twice highlights the *graciousness* of God: the grace He has shown in keeping us this day and begging Him to also show grace in keeping us this night. Between these two reminders of His graciousness falls a petition for the forgiveness of our sin where we have done wrong (including those we are not even aware of). We pray to the Father whose love sent His Son, Jesus Christ, to be our Savior who shed His blood to blot out our sins. Thus, we need not fear that He might say: "You've gone too far this time! No forgiveness for you!" No, we can with confidence and joy commend ourselves body and soul, together with all we love into His loving hands. As we prepare to go to sleep we still ask the company of His angel to protect us from the assaults of the evil one. In the evening, this echoes the traditional prayer from Compline:

> **Visit our dwellings, O Lord, and drive from them all the snares of the enemy;**
> **let Your holy angels dwell with us to preserve us in peace;**
> **and let Your blessing be on us always;**
> **through Jesus Christ, our Lord.**
>
> *—LSB*, p. 257

The final rubric says:

> **Then go to sleep at once and in good cheer.**

No evening hymn unless it be the soft sound of peaceful snoring. You can go to sleep at once and in good cheer because you are a baptized child of God, who has confessed your faith, asked all good things from your Father in heaven, commended all you have and are and love into His loving forgiveness and care, and asked the gift of an angel companion to guard you as you sleep.

You might have noted that the catechism did not seem to have provided a place in the morning and evening prayers for praying for specific needs. Such, however, may easily be enfolded in the Morning or Evening Prayer at this point: "For into Your hands I commend myself, my body and soul"—my wife and children, my neighbor in her sickness—"and all things." You may wish then to make the end of the prayer plural: "Let Your holy angel be with us all, that the evil foe may have no power over any of us. Amen."

Again, just like the Morning Prayer, the Evening Prayer is a prayer habit that takes less than two minutes. By the time you climb into bed, you have had to spend less than four minutes in prayer on a given day to participate in this part of the catechism's training in piety.

Four minutes? Can it really be so simple? Yes, it really can. Just as we can make prayer seem intimidating, we tend to make things far too complicated when it comes to helping our family live in the joys of being children of the heavenly Father. A few minutes of prayer each morning and evening is a great place to begin. The home altar in the morning and the evening is your bed. But the catechism has even more to teach about Daily Prayers.

THE ALTAR OF THE TABLE

—————

HOW THE HEAD OF THE FAMILY SHOULD TEACH HIS HOUSEHOLD TO ASK A BLESSING AND RETURN THANKS.

—The Small Catechism, p. 32

—————

ASKING A BLESSING

The children and members of the household shall go to the table reverently, fold their hands, and say . . .

The catechism wisely injects prayer at the points of our creaturely needs. We need sleep; so prayer frames our lying down and our getting up in the context of our Baptism, using words of Baptism and the sign of the cross. But we also need food. We usually gather around tables in our homes when we eat food.

First, notice that while the Morning and Evening Prayers are essentially individual prayers (since waking up and falling asleep are individual actions), the reception of food is assumed to be a corporate activity. When the food has been readied and set on the table, the children and the members of the household shall go to the table.

I think people to this day resist eating alone. Certainly there are times that it has to be done, but humans seem to intuit deeply that eating alone is missing some essential component. We sense that eating is meant to be an activity we do together, fellow humans sharing the meal. Why, even from birth, eating was corporate! The mother gave the child her breast with its milk. Is this the reason that in homes where a person lives alone, there are virtual people via a television set who become dinner guests of a sort? Without this company, the meal ceases to be communion (a common sharing in) and basically just becomes fodder.

The family comes together, but surely it is striking that they come together *reverently*, even with folded hands. This suggests a recognition of a certain holiness attending our tables and the gifts that are placed upon them. As there is a table in the Church where the family of God gathers to receive a food from the heavenly Father that imparts to them eternal life when it is faithfully received, there is also a table in the home where a smaller family of God gathers to receive a food from the same heavenly Father who sustains also their temporal life. There is no division here between sacred and secular. The Father's giving is what sustains *all* of life, making all of it sacred; and we acknowledge that first and foremost by the way we approach all of the food that He gives. We are not only reverent at the table because we acknowledge that God gives what we receive there but also because life has been given up, whether plants or animals, in order that our life might be sustained a little while longer in this world.

What is implied by our folded hands and our reverence as we gather around the gifts God has given then is made explicit in the words of the liturgy enacted at the table.

. . . and say:

The eyes of all look to You, [O Lord,] and You give them their food at the proper time. You open Your hand and satisfy the desire of every living thing. (Ps. 145:15–16)

Then shall be said the Lord's Prayer and the following:

Lord God, heavenly Father, bless us and these Your gifts which we receive from Your bountiful goodness, through Jesus Christ, our Lord. Amen.

Do you see the parallels between the way the Lord's table is blessed in the Divine Service and the way our tables are blessed at home? We gather around both tables to receive God's gifts. While we are there, the Word of God is proclaimed, telling us who is giving us what. The Lord's Prayer is prayed. Then we pray additionally for a worthy reception of the gifts. And then we simply ask Him to bless us and the gifts we receive through our Lord Jesus.

Even in our homes, then, you might say comes the "distribution," when we actually taste and enjoy our Lord's giving. After we have eaten and been fed, the liturgy at

> DO YOU SEE THE PARALLELS BETWEEN THE WAY THE LORD'S TABLE IS BLESSED IN THE DIVINE SERVICE AND THE WAY OUR TABLES ARE BLESSED AT HOME?

the altar of the home table also sounds like the liturgy at the altar of the Lord's Supper.

RETURNING THANKS

Also, after eating, they shall, in like manner, reverently and with folded hands say:

Give thanks to the Lord, for He is good. His love endures forever. [He] gives food to every creature. He provides food for the cattle and for the young ravens when they call. His pleasure is not in the strength of the horse, nor His delight in the legs of a man; the Lord delights in those who fear Him, who put their hope in His unfailing love. [Ps. 136:1, 25; 147:9–11]

Then shall be said the Lord's Prayer and the following:

We thank You, Lord God, heavenly Father, for all Your benefits, through Jesus Christ, our Lord, who lives and reigns with You and the Holy Spirit forever and ever. Amen.

There are strong echoes here of the post-Communion liturgy. The difference, obviously, at the home altar is that we have not gathered to receive the body and blood of the Savior. Still, we have gathered at a table spread by our heavenly Father with earthly food that was given into death in order that we might go on living by receiving its life into ourselves; therefore, at the altar of our home tables, we give thanks to

Him who lovingly provides us with all that we need to support this body and life.

THE LORD'S PRAYER

We have already noted that the Lord's Prayer is used several times during the Daily Prayers. If one uses it faithfully morning and evening, and asks the blessing and returns thanks at all three meals each day, one ends up reciting the Lord's Prayer at minimum eight times a day. Surely, you might be thinking, "That is a bit much . . . ," no? Yet, the Church's experience with this prayer that Jesus taught us is that we can literally live inside of it all the days of our earthly pilgrimage.

Think of it this way: Is there ever a time when we do not need to remember that we have a Father in heaven who loves us, that we are His true children, and that we can with all boldness and confidence ask anything of Him as His dearly beloved children? Is there really a time that we ought not be asking for His name, which is holy in itself, to be kept holy in our own lives by speech and deed? Is there ever a time when asking for the gift of His kingdom is out of place, since we are actually asking to receive the Holy Spirit that we might believe God's Holy Word and lead godly lives here in time and hereafter in eternity? Ought we not always pray that God's will be done, and is not this very petition the key to peace in our hearts? Is not fretting and anxiety caused by the alternative: fear that our will may not be done? Daily bread includes the food we need, but also so much more. Whenever we sense a lack in any of the things we need for our bodies and lives, ought we not immediately ask the Father? "What father among you, if his son asks for a fish, will instead of a fish give him a serpent; or if he asks for an egg, will give him a scorpion?" (Luke 11:11–12). And asking for forgiveness as we promise to forgive? Is this not a daily need? And also to be preserved in times of temptation and finally delivered from every evil? This prayer really and truly provides the words we fumble for as we try to express the entirety of all of the needs we shall ever face. The

Small Catechism trains us to let the Lord's Prayer's all-encompassing words never be far from our mouth or our heart.

One thing that needs to be addressed here and that has troubled many sensitive consciences is the words our Lord spoke immediately after giving us the "Our Father," which call us back to the Fifth Petition: "For if you forgive others their trespasses, your heavenly Father will also forgive you, but if you do not forgive others their trespasses, neither will your Father forgive your trespasses" (Matthew 6:14–15). Has this ever happened to you? Someone has wronged you or hurt you, and you prayed to God for strength to forgive. You forgave them; but then sometimes months or even years later, you remember what they did and anger or resentment flashes again in your heart. Satan is right there to whisper: "See, you never forgave them! As a result, your own sins are certainly not forgiven." But this is a lie. You did forgive them. But now, as the memory is stirred, God is giving you a great gift. He gives you the opportunity to forgive them yet again, as the assurance that you yourself have been forgiven. The Fifth Petition, as Luther says in the Large Catechism, can thus do everything for you that a sacrament can. You speak aloud that forgiveness one more time, and then your heart is filled with the peace that comes from knowing this is only possible because you yourself have been forgiven.

FROM SET TIMES TO ALL
TIMES AND ALL PLACES

If, as I suggest here, the template of the daily prayers is grounded in Baptism morning and evening (regarding our bed as a type of our tomb from which we rise anew as God's children each morn) and in the Eucharist at meal times (regarding our table as a type of the holy altar where we receive food for which we join in corporate thanksgiving), it then provides a framework for prayer and thanksgiving to spill out over our daily lives. As we confess at the altar each Divine Service, the liturgy teaches us that it is good to give thanks to God "at all times and in all places."

Any person who has ever attempted to help his children memorize the catechism, must surely have spent some time wondering about daily bread. You see, Luther provides a bodaciously long list of all that it includes. Then, he has the nerve at the end to stick in an etcetera: "and the like." He really wasn't trying to torment the youngsters; he *was* giving them a lesson in how impossible it is to number and track all the gifts our loving Father showers on us every single day. Food and drink, yes. But also clothing and shoes (Hermann Sasse once noted that our catechism is the only catechism in the world to mention shoes!), house and home, land and animals, all your goods, a devout (that is, pious!) husband or wife, children and workers, rulers, good government, good weather, peace, health, self-control, good reputation, good friends, faithful neighbors—yes, and the like! In just the same way the catechism opens our understanding of the First Article of the Creed, opening our eyes to see how vast are the gifts that our Father showers upon us, including rescuing us from every evil. Therefore, for all of this it is our duty to "thank and praise, serve and obey Him."

The goal of such catechesis is to train our eyes to actually see what is in front of them, to recognize the hand of the Giver and Protector, to give Him thanks, and then in moments of need, to immediately cry for His help. Luther describes this in the Large Catechism under the Second Commandment:

> **On the other hand, we should also constantly urge and encourage children to honor God's name and to have it constantly on their lips no matter what they meet up with in their experience. . . . Many a frightful, horrible disaster would strike us if God did not preserve us at our calling upon His name. . . . It also helps toward this end if one**

makes it a habit to commit oneself—with soul and body, wife, children, household, and whatever is ours—daily to God's care for every possible eventuality. Thus our custom of praying before and after meals and of having morning and evening prayers arose and continued. In the same way the children's custom originated of making the sign of the cross and saying, "Lord God, save us," "Help, dear Lord Christ," or the like, when they see or hear something frightful and horrible. So, too, on the other hand, when something good—no matter how light—happens unexpectedly to someone, he should say, "God be thanked and praised," "God did this for me," etc. (Janzow 23, 24)

When we are trained to perceive the great gifts that our loving Father provides for us through His Son and by His Spirit, then thanksgiving, intercession, and every form of prayer really do begin to flow naturally in our lives. We learn to sense the Giver behind the countless gifts and to confess our horrid blindness to those gifts apart from His revelation. The simple liturgies of bedside and table provide the framework—the trellis—from which this thanksgiving and intercession naturally and simply bloom forth into our daily lives. Prayer in this manner is not experienced as a burden. In fact, just the opposite! It is rather the growing consciousness that we live our lives in the presence of our most loving God, surrounded by His holy angels, into whose joyful praise we can join our voices at any time.

> THE SIMPLE LITURGIES OF BEDSIDE AND TABLE PROVIDE THE FRAMEWORK—THE TRELLIS—FROM WHICH THIS THANKSGIVING AND INTERCESSION NATURALLY AND SIMPLY BLOOM FORTH INTO OUR DAILY LIVES.

NEVER ALONE

Last, a great joy that we must note about the mystery of our daily prayers: we never pray them alone. The first words of the Lord's Prayer have already shown us this:

Our Father . . .

give *us* . . .

forgive *us* . . .

lead *us* . . .

deliver *us* . . .

Luther once encouraged his barber, Peter, to a more faithful life of prayer by reminding him of this great reality:

Never think that you are kneeling or standing alone, rather think that the whole of Christendom, all devout Christians, are standing there beside you and you are standing among them in a common, united petition which God cannot disdain. (*Treasury of Daily Prayer*, "Writing" from January 4th)

Though we offer our personal prayers, in a strict sense there is no such thing as individual prayer. As we saw in the previous chapter that our personal faith grows out of a corporate experience of the Word, so we also see that personal prayers are always carried along within the whole prayer life of God's people. They are all offered in and through Jesus and so with His whole body, the Church.

Because we pray always together, it is very useful in our daily prayer to explore some of the great prayers that may unite our voices. *Lutheran Service Book* contains many that are worth noting; but one that was particularly near and dear to Luther's heart was the Litany. You can find it on pages 288 and 289. It is a responsive prayer in which the leader begins and others chime in on the response. If you use it to augment your family's prayers (or if you pray it alone, always remembering the whole Church joins with you when you worship), remember it was often used on Wednesdays and Fridays. Why those days? Wednesday in remembrance of Judas' betrayal and fall. Friday in remembrance of our Lord's death. These days are regarded as "penitential" days by the Church, sort of weekly "little Lents" that call us to pray for great, marvelous things.

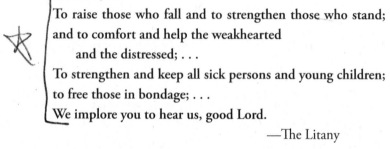

To bring into the way of truth all who have erred and are deceived; . . .
To raise those who fall and to strengthen those who stand; and to comfort and help the weakhearted
and the distressed; . . .
To strengthen and keep all sick persons and young children; to free those in bondage; . . .
We implore you to hear us, good Lord.

—The Litany

It is also a great and godly habit to expand your prayer life during the penitential seasons (Advent and Lent) by regularly using this tremendous prayer.

FOR DISCUSSION

1. What are some of the connections between the daily prayers and Baptism?

keeps us in his faith.

2. In what ways does the catechism teach us to approach our shared mealtimes similarly to the way we approach Holy Communion?

J A God

folded hands & reverance

p. 40 bottom

3. Why is the Lord's Prayer a prayer we could never exhaust or surpass?

p. 43 bottom
& expresses every need we will need

4. How does prayer begin to simply spill out into our lives spontaneously?

a.m + p.m prayers
meal prayer
& give thanks in all times + places

5. What comfort comes from remembering that you never pray alone?

all devout christians are standing with you.

6. When and how might you use the Litany? *p. 48*

Advent, Lent

CHAPTER 3

THE THIRD GODLY HABIT:
Frequent and Faithful Reception of the Eucharist

LORD JESUS CHRIST, YOU HAVE PREPARED
THIS FEAST FOR OUR SALVATION;
IT IS YOUR BODY AND YOUR BLOOD,
AND AT YOUR INVITATION
AS WEARY SOULS, WITH SIN OPPRESSED,
WE COME TO YOU FOR NEEDED REST,
FOR COMFORT AND FOR PARDON.

GRANT THAT WE WORTHILY RECEIVE
YOUR SUPPER, LORD, OUR SAVIOR,
AND, TRULY GRIEVING FOR OUR SINS,
MAY PROVE BY OUR BEHAVIOR
THAT WE ARE THANKFUL FOR YOUR GRACE
AND DAY BY DAY MAY RUN OUR RACE,
IN HOLINESS INCREASING.

—LSB 622:1, 7

WHAT THE EUCHARIST IS AND IS FOR

The third godly habit is the frequent and faithful reception of the Sacrament of the Altar. Before we can discuss why receiving the Lord's

Supper often and in a faith-filled manner is a godly habit, we need to first say clearly what the Lord's Supper is. I have often heard the Sacrament of the Altar, the Eucharist, referred to as an "it" or "thing." But it is much more a "Who." In the Sacrament, we encounter Christ Himself. This is how the Small Catechism says the head of the house should teach the family about this great reality in a very simple way:

What is the Sacrament of the Altar?

It is the true body and blood of our Lord Jesus Christ under the bread and wine, instituted by Christ Himself for us Christians to eat and to drink.

Where is this written?

The holy Evangelists Matthew, Mark, Luke, and St. Paul write: Our Lord Jesus Christ, on the night when He was betrayed, took bread, and when He had given thanks, He broke it and gave it to the disciples and said: "Take, eat; this is My body, which is given for you. This do in remembrance of Me."

In the same way also He took the cup after supper, and when He had given thanks, He gave it to them, saying, "Drink of it, all of you; this cup is the new testament in My blood, which is shed for you for the forgiveness of sins. This do, as often as you drink it, in remembrance of Me."

These words are simple, but they are also profound. They ingeniously allow Jesus Himself to tell us what He gives us in the Sacrament and why He gives it. The catechism calls what He gives us "the true body and blood of our Lord Jesus Christ," and the word "true" here is vital.

It cuts off any attempt to wiggle out of what Jesus actually says: "Take, eat; this is My body, *which is given for you*" and "Drink of it, all of you; this cup is the new testament in My blood, *which is shed for you for the forgiveness of sins.*" He tells us it is His body and it is the body given for us. That would be the same body which was born of the Virgin Mary and was nailed to the cross! He tells us it is His blood, the blood that stained the cross and spilled from wounds and wiped out the sins of the world!

Little children are known for believing what they are told. When it comes to the piety of the Lord's Supper, we need to become little children again; for here Jesus presents us with a mystery which is unfathomable and yet utterly delightful. Here, He takes His own body and blood which He used to win our salvation and imparts them to us to deliver that salvation into us. And He holds it out to us, as the catechism says, "under the bread and wine" and tells us to eat and drink it.

> WHEN IT COMES TO THE PIETY OF THE LORD'S SUPPER, WE NEED TO BECOME LITTLE CHILDREN AGAIN; FOR HERE JESUS PRESENTS US WITH A MYSTERY WHICH IS UNFATHOMABLE AND YET UTTERLY DELIGHTFUL.

Whenever Christians have devoutly pondered the "what" of the Supper, that it is truly the Savior's own body and blood, they have been moved to adoration and prayer. Our *Lutheran Service Book* is chock-full of beautiful hymns contemplating this mystery (see hymns 617–43). One of my favorites is this hymn by Henry Eyster Jacobs:

> Lord Jesus Christ, we humbly pray
> That we may feast on You today;
> Beneath these forms of bread and wine
> Enrich us with Your grace divine.

> Give us, who share this wondrous food,
> Your body broken and Your blood,
> The grateful peace of sins forgiv'n,
> The certain joys of heirs of heav'n.
>
> By faith Your Word has made us bold
> To seize the gift of love retold;
> All that You are we here receive,
> And all we are to You we give.
>
> —*LSB* 623:1–3

Do you hear how the Church in this song confesses that we go to the table not to receive an "it" but a "Him"? It confesses that we feast on Christ, His body and His blood beneath the forms of bread and wine. Another one of our hymns reminds us about the altar, "Here, O my Lord, I see Thee face to face; Here would I touch and handle things unseen" (*LSB* 631:1).

A childlike faith will take the Lord Jesus at His Word. This is the faith that Lutherans have always had concerning the Lord's Supper and, in this, they are solidly in the stream of the historic Church's confession. The overwhelming majority of Christians across the centuries have happily and boldly ventured to believe that Jesus meant what He said and said what He meant when He instituted His Supper. With them, we Lutherans believe that we actually eat and drink Christ's true body and blood.

But why did Christ give us this gift and command us to "do it" "often" "in remembrance of" Him? The Small Catechism turns to that next:

What is the benefit of this eating and drinking?

These words, "Given and shed for you for the forgiveness of sins," show us that in the Sacrament forgiveness of sins, life,

and salvation are given us through these words. For where there is forgiveness of sins, there is also life and salvation.

The words of Jesus, "Given and shed for you for the forgiveness of sins," disclose to us why He imparts His body and blood in the Eucharist. Christians have sometimes been confused about an important distinction here: the difference between how salvation was won and how salvation is bestowed. There is no question that the salvation of the world was accomplished by our Lord as He offered His body and His blood, His very self, once and for all through the Eternal Spirit to the Father on Calvary's cross. The author to the Hebrews emphasized this:

> *And every priest stands daily at His service, offering repeatedly the same sacrifices, which can never take away sins. But when Christ had offered for all time a single sacrifice for sins, He sat down at the right of hand of God, waiting from that time until His enemies should be made a footstool for His feet. For by a single offering He has perfected for all time those who are being sanctified. . . . Where there is forgiveness of these, there is no longer any offering for sin.* (Hebrews 10:11–14, 18)

But if salvation was accomplished by the Savior on Golgotha and if His Father showed His approval by raising Jesus from the dead, how is that salvation accessible to us now? Some of our Protestant friends like to sing a hymn that says: "There is power, power, wonder-working power in the blood of the Lamb."[3] We'd agree. There is! But we'd also ask: "And where would I happen to find that blood?" In the Eucharist, at His Altar, the Crucified and Risen Savior imparts the salvation that

---

3. This hymn appears with various titles including "Power in the Blood." It has been attributed to Lewis Edgar Jones and is in public domain.

He won by His once-for-all sacrifice on the cross. I don't think we have a clearer confession of this in our hymnal than *LSB* 534. Think about these words:

> **Though the lowliest form now veil You**
> **As of old in Bethlehem,**
> **Here as there Your angels hail You,**
> **Branch and flow'r of Jesse's stem.**
> **Alleluia, alleluia, alleluia!**
> **We in worship join with them;**
> **We in worship join with them.**
>
> **Paschal Lamb, Your off'ring, finished**
> **Once for all when You were slain,**
> **In its fullness undiminished**
> **Shall forevermore remain,**
> **Alleluia, alleluia, alleluia!**
> **Cleansing souls from ev'ry stain;**
> **Cleansing souls from ev'ry stain.**
>
> *—LSB* 534:2–3

The sacrifice was offered only one time to the Father, and yet in the Sacrament, the living Lord comes to us every time with the very body and blood that were the ransom price of our bodies and souls; through them, He gives us His forgiveness. And, "where there is forgiveness of sins, there is also life and salvation."

God's own life comes to you wrapped in this forgiveness. Think of electricity. Is it a good thing or a bad thing? If you didn't have a protective cord around the wires and tried to warm yourself by grabbing hold of the current flowing through the wires, you *would* become warm—but not in a good way. Our living God is like that. Because of our sin, if He were to give Himself to us directly, we would perish as quickly as Uzzah did when he reached out an unauthorized hand

and touched the ark of the covenant (see 2 Samuel 6:5–9). But God provides a way to wrap Himself up in His forgiveness and impart to us a share in His own divine life; and the way that He wraps Himself up to come to us is through Jesus' body and blood. Jesus hinted at this miracle in John 6 when He said, "Whoever feeds on My flesh and drinks My blood abides in Me, and I in him. As the living Father sent Me, and I live because of the Father, so whoever feeds on Me, he also will live because of Me" (John 6:56–57). Where the Son of God comes to you in love, gives you forgiveness, and pours into you His divine life from the Father, there you also discover salvation. Salvation *is* communion with the Father through the Son in the Holy Spirit. This is what we were made for; it is what we fell from, what Christ came to restore—and what the Holy Spirit delights to deliver to us.

But all of that is a pretty tall order. Are we actually saying that eating and drinking can do such great things? Before we answer, you might ponder that it was by eating that a "great thing" was done in Genesis 3: sin and death came into this world through food going into human mouths. Is it so odd, then, that deliverance from sin and death should also come through eating and drinking?

The catechism addresses the question by reminding us that, as always, man does not live by bread alone, but by every word that proceeds from the mouth of God:

How can bodily eating and drinking do such great things?

Certainly not just eating and drinking do these things, but the words written here: "Given and shed for you for the forgiveness of sins." These words, along with the bodily eating and drinking, are the main thing in the Sacrament. Whoever believes these words has exactly what they say: "forgiveness of sins."

Eve divorced eating from the word of God, and the result was death and sin. Jesus in the Eucharist reunites eating and drinking with the word of God, and the result is that whoever believes has exactly what God's words say: forgiveness! If you didn't have the words that told you why Jesus was giving you His body and blood, you would have a treasure that you would not know how to open or use. When He says that it is for the forgiveness of your sins, you then know how it may be properly received: in faith, with thanksgiving and praise. He gives it to you as the promise that your sins are forgiven and gone.

> IF YOU THINK ABOUT THE GREAT GIFT HERE SHARED, THERE WILL NEVER BE A NEED FOR SOMEONE TO BADGER AND HOUND YOU INTO GOING TO THE SACRAMENT.

If you think about the great gift here shared, there will never be a need for someone to badger and hound you into going to the Sacrament. You'll come running to church begging your pastor for it, as Luther describes in the Large Catechism:

Never regard the Sacrament as something harmful from which to flee, but rather as purely wholesome and soothing therapy that is helpful and life-giving both for the soul and for the body. For if the soul is healed, the body is helped as well. How, then, is it that we act as if the Sacrament were a poison and eating it would kill us? . . . But those who feel their weakness, really want to be rid of it, and desire a remedy should regard and use the Sacrament as a priceless antidote against the poison that they carry in them. For here in the Sacrament you receive from the lips of Christ forgiveness of sins, and His forgiveness contains and brings with it God's grace, God's Spirit, all the gifts of the Spirit, and His protection shielding and sheltering you against death, the devil, and all evil. (Janzow 119)

At the same time, however, Lutherans have always been careful not to make laws about how often a person ought to receive this incredible gift. The Large Catechism deals with this when it warns us not to regard receiving it as a burden or work, nor, conversely, to regard the gift as unimportant for our lives (leading us to neglect it). The very word "ought" makes us concerned that we are trying to turn something that is a free gift of love from God into a work we are doing for God.

It is of course true what we said, that nobody should ever be driven or forced to attend the Lord's Supper, lest a new slaughter of souls begin. We must nevertheless understand that people who absent themselves and abstain for such long periods of time from the Sacrament are not to be taken for Christians. For Christ did not institute it to be treated as a spectator drama, but has commanded His Christians to eat and to drink, and to remember Him as they do so.

True Christians who prize and cherish the Sacrament should indeed motivate and urge themselves to fill the Communion tables. (Janzow 115)

So no one can make a rule about how often you should receive Holy Communion. Our Lutheran Confessions assume that in our Churches, the Sacrament is offered each Sunday and feast day (a practice which is becoming more common among Missouri Synod congregations again—a very welcome development). Our Confessions never assert that just because the Sacrament is offered, everyone present should feel constrained to receive it. In fact, our Confessions assume that no one will commune who has not taken time to examine himself or herself in order to ensure that he or she is receiving the Sacrament in a worthy manner. As St. Paul exhorted in 1 Corinthians 11:28, "Let a person examine himself, then, and so eat of the bread and drink of the cup."

Who receives this sacrament worthily?

Fasting and bodily preparation are certainly fine outward training. But that person is truly worthy and well prepared who has faith in these words: "Given and shed for you for the forgiveness of sins."

But anyone who does not believe these words or doubts them is unworthy and unprepared, for the words "for you" require all hearts to believe.

Let's not pass too quickly by the "fasting and bodily preparation" that are "certainly fine outward training." The very way these are spoken of suggests that they are valuable, even if they do not by themselves provide complete preparation. Fasting, of course, means going without food. Christians in years gone by would regularly withhold food from their bodies until they had partaken in church of the food for their soul, Christ's body and blood, on any day they planned to commune. My wife and I adopted this practice a long time ago, but I must confess it had a side effect we actually hadn't anticipated. Not worrying about preparing, eating, and cleaning up food on Sunday mornings makes time and space for you to approach the Service peacefully. We only had to shower and dress (part of the "bodily preparation," one could argue). Breaking our nighttime fast with a feast of God's Word and the Holy Eucharist reminds us precisely that our life isn't sustained by bread alone, but by every word from the mouth of God. Including the word, "Take and eat!"

This can be a very beneficial practice, but still, it is not the most important part of being "well prepared" to worthily receive the Eucharist. The catechism says a "person is truly worthy and well prepared who has faith in these words: 'Given and shed for you for the forgiveness of sins.'" Isn't it odd that Luther didn't say "who has faith in 'This is my Body, . . . my Blood'"? The point here is that though asserting correct dogmatic teachings is in theory good, it is not enough until you believe and confess that they are correct and true *for you*. That is faith, in fact: making plural pronouns singular! Paul did this for the Galatians. He began by proclaiming, "Grace to you and peace from God our Father and the Lord Jesus Christ, who gave Himself for our sins to deliver us from the present evil age, according to the will of our God and Father" (Galatians 1:3–4). All true. But then Paul switched the pronouns, as an example of what faith proclaims: "It is no longer I who live, but Christ who lives in me. And the life I now live in the flesh I live by faith in the Son of God, *who loved me and gave Himself for me*" (Galatians 2:20, emphasis added).

When you approach the Sacrament in a worthy manner, it means you are approaching it hearing Jesus say that He is giving *you* the body He gave for *you;* the blood He shed for *you,* for the forgiveness of *your* sin. The most awful way we could abuse the Sacrament would be to come to it calling Jesus a liar, saying that what He says isn't true at all. The catechism warns someone who does not believe Jesus' words, then, to stay away.

Rather than thoughtlessly getting in line because the Sacrament is offered, a faithful reception of the Lord's Supper stops to ponder exactly what is being offered and why it is being offered and how very much I need what is so graciously given. A faithful reception is the opposite of automatic or unthinking; rather, it is intentional and deliberate. Examine yourself; ask yourself: why am I coming to Communion? What exactly does Jesus give me there? Why does He give it to me? Why do I need such a gift?

However, the catechism's insistence on self-examination does not mean, as we sometimes erroneously conclude, that we should not come if we feel unworthy. In the Large Catechism, Luther teaches us:

But suppose you say, "What if I feel unfit?" Answer: I am tempted the same way, which is a carry-over from our former situation under the pope. . . . We all became so timid that we easily took fright and would say, "O how unfit I am." At that point human nature and reason begin to measure our unworthiness against the greatness of the Sacrament's priceless treasure, in comparison with which our unrighteousness seems like a smoke-darkened lantern in the brightness of the sun, or like junk in comparison with jewelry. Nature and reason, seeing this contrast, keep people from going to the Sacrament until they feel more prepared. But one week becomes another, and one half-year leads to the next. If you insist on weighing how good and pure you are and if you wait until you feel no stings of conscience, you will never approach the Lord's Table.

We must therefore make a distinction between people. The rude and disorderly are to be told to stay away, for they are not fit to receive the forgiveness of sins because they do not desire it and do not want to lead a good life. As for the rest who are not such coarse and loose-living people and would like to live right, they should not stay away even if they are spiritually weak and sickly. . . . For no one will ever reach a level where he no longer has the many common defects in his blood and flesh.

People who are troubled about this should learn that the highest wisdom is the realization that this sacrament does not depend on our worthiness. . . . We come as poor, miserable humans precisely because we are unworthy, unless there be someone who desires no grace and absolution nor intends to amend his life. (Janzow 117–18)

CHRISTIAN QUESTIONS WITH THEIR ANSWERS

Lutherans developed a number of resources to help Christians examine themselves and thus prepare to receive the Sacrament in a worthy manner. Luther's own is often appended to the catechism: "The Christian Questions with their Answers."

PREPARED BY DR. MARTIN LUTHER FOR THOSE WHO INTEND TO GO TO THE SACRAMENT.

After confession and instruction in the Ten Commandments, the Creed, the Lord's Prayer, and the Sacraments of Baptism and the Lord's Supper, the pastor may ask, or Christians may ask themselves these questions:

1. Do you believe that you are a sinner?
Yes, I believe it. I am a sinner.

2. How do you know this?
From the Ten Commandments, which I have not kept.

3. Are you sorry for your sins?
Yes, I am sorry that I have sinned against God.

4. What have you deserved from God because of your sins?
His wrath and displeasure, temporal death, and eternal damnation. See Rom. 6:21, 23.

5. Do you hope to be saved?
Yes, that is my hope.

6. In whom then do you trust?

In my dear Lord Jesus Christ.

7. Who is Christ?

The Son of God, true God and man.

8. How many Gods are there?

Only one, but there are three persons: Father, Son, and Holy Spirit.

9. What has Christ done for you that you trust in Him?

He died for me and shed His blood for me on the cross for the forgiveness of sins.

10. Did the Father also die for you?

He did not. The Father is God only, as is the Holy Spirit; but the Son is both true God and true man. He died for me and shed His blood for me.

11. How do you know this?

From the holy Gospel, from the words instituting the Sacrament, and by His body and blood given me as a pledge in the Sacrament.

12. What are the words of institution?

Our Lord Jesus Christ, on the night when He was betrayed, took bread, and when He had given thanks, He broke it and gave it to the disciples and said: "Take eat; this is My body, which is given for you. This do in remembrance of Me."

In the same way also He took the cup after supper, and when He had given thanks, He gave it to them, saying: "Drink of it, all of you; this cup is the new testament in My blood, which is

shed for you for the forgiveness of sins. This do,
as often as you drink it, in remembrance of Me."

13. **Do you believe, then, that the true body and blood of Christ are in the Sacrament?**
    Yes, I believe it.

14. **What convinces you to believe this?**
    The word of Christ: Take, eat, this is My body;
    drink of it, all of you, this is My blood.

15. **What should we do when we eat His body and drink His blood, and in this way receive His pledge?**
    We should remember and proclaim His death
    and the shedding of His blood, as He taught
    us: This do, as often as you drink it, in remem-
    brance of Me.

16. **Why should we remember and proclaim His death?**
    First, so that we may learn to believe that no crea-
    ture could make satisfaction for our sins. Only
    Christ, true God and man, could do that. Sec-
    ond, so we may learn to be horrified by our sins,
    and to regard them as very serious. Third, so we
    may find joy and comfort in Christ alone, and
    through faith in Him be saved.

17. **What motivated Christ to die and make full payment for your sins?**
    His great love for His Father and for me and
    other sinners, as it is written in John 14; Romans
    5; Galatians 2; and Ephesians 5.

18. **Finally, why do you wish to go to the Sacrament?**

   That I may learn to believe that Christ, out of great love, died for my sin, and also learn from Him to love God and my neighbor.

19. **What should admonish and encourage a Christian to receive the Sacrament frequently?**

   First, both the command and the promise of Christ the Lord. Second, his own pressing need, because of which the command, encouragement, and promise are given.

20. **But what should you do if you are not aware of this need and have no hunger and thirst for the Sacrament?**

   To such a person no better advice can be given than this: first, he should touch his body to see if he still has flesh and blood. Then he should believe what the Scriptures say of it in Galatians 5 and Romans 7. Second, he should look around to see whether he is still in the world, and remember that there will be no lack of sin and trouble, as the Scriptures say in John 15–16 and in 1 John 2 and 5.

   Third, he will certainly have the devil also around him, who with his lying and murdering day and night will let him have no peace, within or without, as the Scriptures picture him in John 8 and 16; 1 Peter 5; Ephesians 6; and 2 Timothy 2.

Note: These questions and answers are no child's play, but are drawn up with great earnestness of purpose by the

venerable and devout Dr. Luther for both young and old.
Let each one pay attention and consider it a serious matter; for St. Paul writes to the Galatians in chapter 6: "Do
not be deceived: God cannot be mocked."

It is a beneficial practice to read through these questions regularly,
maybe as often as once a month. A good time to do so is a Saturday
evening when you plan on communing the next day. Or, if you have
a few moments before the Divine Service begins, open your hymnal
and review them. You can find them in *Lutheran Service Book* on pages
329–30.

PRAYERS FOR MEDITATION ON THE EUCHARIST

The first page inside the hymnal also provides a prayer that can be
offered before communing. I'd like to offer a few others that I have
found helpful in my own preparation for receiving the Eucharist:

St. John Chrysostom

Know, O Lord my God, I am unworthy that You should
enter beneath the roof of the temple of my soul, because it
is all empty and dead. There is in me no worthy place where
You may lay Your head. But since from Your loftiness You
humbled Yourself for our sake, please humble Yourself now
toward my humility. And as it seemed good to You to lie in
the cavern and in the manger of dumb beasts, so also now
graciously lie in the manger of my dumb soul, and enter
into my defiled body. Just as You did not refuse to enter into
the house of Simon the leper, and there to sit at a meal with
sinners, so also graciously enter into the house of my humble soul, which is leprous and sinful. Just as You did not

feel loathing for the polluted lips of a sinful woman who kissed Your feet, so also do not loathe my even more defiled and polluted lips and unclean tongue. Amen. (*Treasury of Daily Prayer*, p. 1445)

Johann Starck

My Jesus, how can I ever sufficiently praise Your great love? You have not only given Yourself into death for me, a poor sinner, but also have ordained Your holy body and Your precious blood as the food for my soul in the Holy Supper. O Love, Your death brings me life. Your body and Your blood strengthen and refresh me unto the life that never ends. By this means I abide in You and You in me; You live in me and I obtain righteousness and strength in You. Therefore, my sin cannot frighten me, and Satan cannot condemn me. In this gracious feast I receive the ransom for my sins. Here, I receive the body that was given into death for me. Here, I receive the blood that was shed for me for the forgiveness of my sin. This is the blood of atonement by which my sins and the sins of all people have been canceled. Now, as surely as I receive it, so surely God is merciful to me, and I have the forgiveness of all my sins. In Holy Baptism, the first sacrament I received, You gave me a new life in the Holy Spirit, thus assuring me that I am Your child and heir. In the Holy Supper, the ongoing sacrament, You give me the pledge of Your body and blood to preserve and strengthen in me the new life.

O my God, sanctify my soul, strengthen my faith, that I may receive this feast of love worthily and for my salvation. Grant that my thoughts may always be with You. Drive from my heart all sinful suggestions, desires, and anything that might hinder my devotion, that You may abide in me, and that I may be and abide in You to all eternity. Amen. (*Starck's Prayer Book*, p. 156)

JOHANN STARCK

O Jesus, now that I am to partake of Your holy feast of love, I receive it also in remembrance of You. I remember Your love, how for my sake You came into the world to make me an heir of life everlasting. I remember Your anguish, pain, and wounds by which my sins and punishments have been removed from me and Your righteousness bestowed on me. I remember Your death and Your resurrection by which life and salvation have been imparted to me. I know, O Jesus, that for Your sake I obtain grace, sonship, peace, and heaven's joy. I shall not be lost if I abide in You, O Jesus, and You abide in me.

O abide, then, in my heart. Dwell in my heart, live and run in it. Let me be Yours now and for eternity. Let Your holy body be my food, Your holy blood my drink, and refresh me unto life everlasting. Grant that I may never lose this treasure, but that You, my Jesus, henceforth may live, rule, and dwell in me. Israel's manna had to be gathered in a clean vessel. Oh, that You would then purify my heart by true faith, genuine repentance, love, and humility, so that I may worthily receive this pledge of Your love and constantly keep it for the strengthening of my faith, the sanctification of my life, and the assurance of my salvation. O precious Holy Spirit, preserve me in this grace unto my blessed end. Guard me, lest I again sin wantonly and fall from grace, and my last condition be worse than the first. Until death let me continue in faith in the triune God, in love toward my neighbor, and in godliness, that I may obtain the end of faith, the salvation of my soul. (*Starck's Prayer Book*, pp. 157–58)

David Hollaz

Almighty Lord Jesus Christ, source of life and immortality, I pray and implore You as devoutly as I can to enlighten my mind, full of native shadows as it is, with Your most Holy Spirit. . . . As often as I shall come to Your holy table to refresh my spirit, I pray You to make me, unworthy as I am, worthy through Your grace; impure as I am to make me clean; naked as I am to clothe me, so that Your body, so full of divine power, and Your most precious blood, may not become for me, Your servant, the occasion for judgment or punishment, but a memorial of the death You underwent for me, a strengthening of my faith, a proof of the taking away of my sins, a bond of closer union with You, an increase of holiness, the basis of a glad resurrection, and a pledge of everlasting life. Amen. (Cited by Arthur Carl Piepkorn in *The Church*, p. 157.)

Prayers at the Distribution:

Before receiving the Lord's body

> Lord, I am not worthy to have You come under the roof of my soul, but only say the Word and Your servant shall be healed. Amen. (adapted from Matthew 8:8)

Before receiving the Lord's blood

> I will lift up the cup of salvation and call on the name of the Lord. I will call upon the Lord, who is worthy to be praised, and I am saved from my enemies. Amen. (Psalm 116:13; Psalm 18:3)

My own Prayer after Receiving the Sacrament:

> O Lord Jesus Christ, I thank You that You have permitted me, Your unworthy servant, to partake of this, Your most holy body and precious blood. I beg that it may be to me for the forgiveness of all my sins, for strength in resisting temptations, for service in Your kingdom, and finally for the glories of the life that has no end. Glory to You, Lord Jesus Christ, my King and my God. Glory to You forever! Amen.

There are many, many more that could be cited from Lutheran prayer books and hymnals, but I point these out merely because I have found these to be beneficial before communing. Another of my favorite ways to prepare to receive the Sacrament is to open up the hymnal and meditate on several of the hymns in the "Lord's Supper" section. In *Lutheran Service Book*, that covers hymns 617–43. Two of those hymns which Lutherans of old used repeatedly are 617, "O Lord, We Praise Thee," and 627, "Jesus Christ, Our Blessed Savior." The first was adapted by Martin Luther from a medieval hymn, and the second is Luther's adaptation of a hymn by John Hus. However you prepare to go to the Lord's Supper, time spent in prayer before and in thanksgiving after can be a very beneficial habit.

This section would be incomplete without a word about etiquette when visiting a congregation that is not your own on a day you wish to commune. First, as Lutherans, we only commune at congregations that share the same confession of the faith that we ourselves have professed. Second, we never just show up and make our way to the altar, unannounced. Rather, it is best to arrive at the church early enough to find the pastor, introduce yourself, and indicate your desire to receive Communion that day. He may ask you something like: "Tell me why you want to commune today? Where do you regularly worship?" "What do you believe you receive at the altar?" and so on. If for any reason a suspicion arises in your own mind that the confession of the Sacrament at that place is different from your own, feel free to ask *him*: "So what is it that you hold in your hand and place into my mouth?" (Luther gave this advice in an open letter to the Christians of Frankfurt about what to do if something seemed fishy in a church's celebration of the Sacrament.) If he can't say, "Christ's body and blood for the forgiveness of your sins," it is best not to commune there, even if you would be welcomed to the table.

Last but not least: when you bring a first-time visitor with you to church, the Sacrament is being celebrated, and you know that your visitor is not a Lutheran, has not been instructed in the catechism, and has never made a public profession of the faith we confess, you have a job to do. It is your job to tell your visitor upfront and before arriving at church that our church does not commune any Christian who has not been examined and absolved, and who has not publicly confessed the same Lutheran understanding of the Christian faith (usually by rite of Confirmation). There is no need to attempt to justify this to your visitor; they will respect you all the more if you simply explain that this is the practice of the congregation they are visiting.

For Discussion

1. What difference is there in how you think about and treat Holy Communion if you regard the Sacrament as an "it," a "something," rather than as an encounter with the living Lord in His true body and blood?

encounter Christ himself.

2. Why do Lutherans believe, along with most Christians, that in the Eucharist we actually receive the true body and blood of Christ?

what he gives and why. true body + blood.

3. What is the connection between eating and sin, and eating and salvation?

where there is salvation, there is forgiveness

4. Why does Christ wish us to receive the Sacrament?

eat + drink + remember Christ

5. Should you stay away from the Sacrament if you feel unworthy? Why or why not?

does not depend on worthiness.

6. What causes someone to receive the Sacrament unworthily?

7. What helps or resources have you used to prepare for a reverent and joyful reception of Christ's body and blood?

meditate on old hymns.

CHAPTER 4

THE FOURTH GODLY HABIT:
Confession of Sins and Absolution

—————✣————

LORD, TO YOU I MAKE CONFESSION:
I HAVE SINNED AND GONE ASTRAY,
I HAVE MULTIPLIED TRANSGRESSION,
CHOSEN FOR MYSELF MY WAY.

LED BY YOU TO SEE MY ERRORS,
LORD, I TREMBLE AT YOUR TERRORS.

LORD, ON YOU I CAST MY BURDEN—
SINK IT IN THE DEEPEST SEA!

LET ME KNOW YOUR GRACIOUS PARDON,
CLEANSE ME FROM INIQUITY.

LET YOUR SPIRIT LEAVE ME NEVER;
MAKE ME ONLY YOURS FOREVER.

—*LSB* 608:1, 4

—————✣————

Christians speak about their own sin. The word *confess* means to speak the same thing as God does about our sin. To confess sins is thus more than acknowledging that we feel badly, that we have done something wrong, or that we have failed to do something right. To confess our sins is to acknowledge before God the truth that He has declared in His Word about us, our sins, and what our sins have deserved and demanded.

PUBLIC CONFESSION

When we come together for the Divine Service, the first order of business after an opening hymn and the Invocation is usually this Confession. In Divine Service, Settings One and Two, we hear words similar to 1 John 1:8–9: "If we say we have no sin, we deceive ourselves, and the truth is not in us. But if we confess our sins, God, who is faithful and just, will forgive our sins and cleanse us from all unrighteousness" (*LSB*, pp. 151, 167). In these words, we learn a very important fact about Confession: what frees us to actually own up to the mess we are and the messes we have made in our lives is that the One before whom we confess is a divine ever-flowing spring of forgiveness and mercy. Psalm 103 celebrates this with joy:

> *The LORD is merciful and gracious, slow to anger and abounding in steadfast love. He will not always chide, nor will He keep His anger forever. He does not deal with us according to our sins, nor repay us according to our iniquities. For as high as the heavens are above the earth, so great is His steadfast love toward those who fear Him; as far as the east is from the west, so far does He remove our transgressions from us. As a father shows compassion to his children, so the LORD shows compassion to those who fear Him. For He knows our frame; He remembers that we are dust. (Psalm 103:8–14)*

It is in the warmth of God's steadfast, unshakable love that we can gain the courage to be honest before Him. He delights to forgive and yearns to speak His pardon to us. This is what frees us to drop the fig leaves and stand exposed before Him.

In Divine Service, Setting Three, the words of Psalm 32:5 invite us to see the same graciousness on God's part: "I said, I will confess my transgressions unto the Lord, and You forgave the iniquity of my sin." And in Divine Service, Setting Four, it is the words of Psalm 130:3–4: "If You, O Lord,

> IT IS IN THE WARMTH OF GOD'S STEADFAST, UNSHAKABLE LOVE THAT WE CAN GAIN THE COURAGE TO BE HONEST BEFORE HIM. HE DELIGHTS TO FORGIVE AND YEARNS TO SPEAK HIS PARDON TO US. THIS IS WHAT FREES US TO DROP THE FIG LEAVES AND STAND EXPOSED BEFORE HIM.

kept a record of sins, O Lord, who could stand? But with You there is forgiveness; therefore You are feared." In each instance, we are comforted by the promise of forgiveness and God's welcome before we dare to speak the truth about ourselves that we learn from the Word of God.

The confessions we use in our Church are brutally honest. Let the import of these words sink in:

We are by nature sinful and unclean. We have sinned against You in thought, word, and deed, by what we have done and by what we have left undone. We have not loved You with our whole heart; we have not loved our neighbors as ourselves. We justly deserve Your present and eternal punishment. (Divine Service, Settings One and Two)

I, a poor, miserable sinner, confess unto You all my sins and iniquities with which I have ever offended You and justly deserved Your temporal and eternal punishment. (Divine Service, Settings Three and Five)

We poor sinners confess unto You that we are by nature sinful and unclean and that we have sinned against You by thought, word, and deed. (Divine Service, Setting Three)

Let us first consider our unworthiness and confess before God and one another that we have sinned in thought, word, and deed, and that we cannot free ourselves from this sinful condition. (Divine Service, Setting Four)

The language of "by nature" requires some unpacking. At the time of the Reformation, there were folks who wanted to stress so much the corruption of our nature, they identified human nature itself with sin. To be human, in their thought, equaled to be sinful. Our Confessions flat out reject this identification as contradicting the Scriptures. Our human nature is not itself sin. Christ did not assume sin. He did not redeem sin. He will not glorify sin. But He did assume a human nature. He redeemed and healed our human nature. At His appearing, He will glorify our nature by raising our bodies from death and making them incorruptible.

So what do we mean when we say that we are sinful by nature? Think of sin as a horrid corruption that has spread itself like a Stage 4 cancer all through our human nature. It affects every bit of us: our desiring, our thinking, our physical appetites, and our emotions. Only God is able to zap the corruption and salvage the nature; to do so ourselves is utterly impossible. But the cancer *isn't* the body; it's a corruption *in* the body. In just the same way, the sin that infects us body and soul, inside and out, since the fall and which is passed on to each of us simply by being conceived of fallen flesh and blood, this sin is not us. Nevertheless, it thoroughly infects and corrupts us.

And this point is vital. We need to be clear that this corruption is not something that results from us sinning; that has it exactly backwards. The sin that shows up in our actions or our failures to act in thought, word, or deed springs from the corruption in which we were conceived. David confesses this in Psalm 51:5, "Behold, I was brought forth in iniquity and in sin did my mother conceive me." St. Paul reinforces this when he writes in Ephesians 2:1–3:

> *And you were dead in the trespasses and sins in which you once walked, following the course of this world, following the prince of the power of the air, the spirit that is now at work in the sons of disobedience—among whom we all once lived in the passions of our flesh, carrying out the desires of the body and the mind, and were* BY NATURE *children of wrath, like the rest of mankind. (emphasis added)*

Any parent knows this truth if they simply think about their children. No child has to be taught to be selfish or demanding. We come out of the womb that way! The cutest little bundle that looks so sweet and innocent in its mother's arms still fully bears this corruption in its nature. Give it time and this corruption manifests itself. This corruption is the result of the fall of Adam and Eve; this result is described in devastating words in Genesis 6:5: "The Lord saw that the wickedness of man was great in the earth, and that every intention of the thoughts of his heart was only evil continually." That sounds so bad we think it surely can't be right. Is it an exaggeration? Sadly not. It is the truth. Each one of us comes into this world with a twisted and distorted interior perspective, viewing ourselves as the center of the universe—the place that only God can justly claim. Put together a bunch of people who each think everything revolves around them and you get the mess you can read about in the paper, on your smartphone, or even in your own heart.

In fact, since the fall of our first parents, only one human being has been born who fully possessed human nature, but without any corruption: Jesus Christ. Only our Savior by His miraculous incarnation in the Virgin Mother by the power of the Holy Spirit had a human nature that was without sin. And the ironic thing is, He, being true God, really was the center of the universe! But look at Him closely; see how every natural notion we have about God is wrong. He comes among us not proud, but humble. Not to be served, but to serve and give His life as a ransom for many.

So when we confess that we are by nature sinful, we are saying what the Word of God declares to be true about our fallen human nature. We are in effect saying not that we are sinners because we sin, but rather that we sin because we are sinners.

Furthermore, one sure sign of the corruption of our nature is that none of us wants to think that our own sins are all that bad. In the public Confession, we dare to say quite the opposite. We sweep all our sins into a big pile, including those we are not even aware of. We pronounce over that heaping, stinking mess the verdict that God's own Word pronounces upon it. We freely admit that by our sin we have justly deserved God's temporal and eternal punishment. Unlike the spoiled child who cries out, "But that's not fair!" we acknowledge that it would be entirely fair for God to visit all manner of punishments on us not only in this life but also to send us to eternal damnation in the age to come. We fess up that we deserve nothing less.

Now this is not a perspective anyone would ever arrive at by just using their own brains. It is something God has to reveal to us in His Word. Apart from that Word and, in particular, the brutally honest mirror of His Law, we tend to abide in the false security that while we may not be the greatest folks in the world, we surely do not deserve all manner of hardship now and certainly not the unending fire of hell later. Because it goes down deep and exposes the depths of our hearts, the Word discloses to us the corruption of sin in our nature. It opens our eyes to see the terrifying reality we are actually in.

A quick word on the difference between a terrified conscience and a troubled one.[4] After Adam and Eve ate what God had forbidden, they had troubled consciences. How do we know? Look at what they did! They made fig leaf aprons for themselves. They knew something was wrong, and it bothered them; so they tried to fix it. Their consciences were troubled, not at rest. And that is the state of many people in this world. They know that they have screwed up. They admit as much. They have a vague uneasiness about the situation and continually try new ways to solve it. Fig leaf fashion is still all the rage. Check out the self-help section of your local bookstore. You'll see how little we've changed. "If only I fix my diet, my finances, my relationships, my body . . ."; the list goes on and on.

But when God appears on the scene as He does in the Garden of Eden, the truth comes home: those pitiful fig leaves cannot shield one blasted thing from His all-seeing eyes. His very presence blows them away. How did the writer to the Hebrews put it? "All are naked and exposed to the eyes of Him to whom we must give account" (Hebrews 4:13). The presence of God gave Adam and Eve the gift of terrified consciences in the place of their troubled ones; and so they ran! They ran in terror to the trees and tried in vain to hide. The only tree that the terrified conscience *can* hide behind is the cross; but Adam and

---

4. Thanks to Pastor Bryan Wolfmueller for teaching me this!

Eve do not know that yet. All they know now is that God has come to call them to account, and there is nothing they can do to fix the mess they have made. There is nothing they can do to fix the even worse mess that they have now become inside and out, through and through. This is reflected in their shattered trust of each other. Adam's corrupted vision sees the good gift of the woman in whom he had earlier delighted now only as a snare set by God ("the woman You gave me!") and the reason for their disobedience. When Eve is thrown under the bus by the man who had failed to protect her, her corrupted vision tries to keep passing the blame along; she blames God in a subtler way, fixing the blame for her actions on the serpent. Guilty on the inside before God, they both attempt to shift the focus somewhere, anywhere else! Their consciences are terrified indeed.

Jesus said, "You will know the truth, and the truth will set you free" (John 8:32). And how do you come to know the truth? "If you abide in My word" (John 8:31). Abiding in that Word makes you see the truth. The first part of the truth is the devastating revelation of our sin and the wrath of God against all ungodliness and unrighteousness of men (see Romans 1:18). The Law robs you of excuses. It silences the blame game. No more, "The woman You gave me . . ."; the serpent deceived me. . . ." It makes us see that we are all locked up in the same prison and that we can do absolutely nothing to get out of it. Listen to St. Paul's sweeping indictment in Romans 3:

> *For we have already charged that all, both Jews and Greeks, are under the power of sin, as it is written:*

> **"None is righteous, no, not one;**
>   **no one understands;**
>   **no one seeks for God.**

All have turned aside; together they have become worth-
less;
>no one does good, not even one."
"Their throat is an open grave;
>they use their tongues to deceive."
"The venom of asps is under their lips."
>"Their mouth is full of curses and bitterness."
"Their feet are swift to shed blood;
>in their paths are ruin and misery,
and the way of peace they have not known."
>"There is no fear of God before their eyes."

Now we know that whatever the law says it speaks to those who are under the law, so that every mouth may be stopped, and the whole world may be held accountable to God. For by works of the law no human being will be justified in His sight, since through the law comes knowledge of sin. (Romans 3:9b–20)

That is you. And that is me. That is every last human being. This is a hard truth. Sin corrupts our nature and shows up in the various sins of our life. But all these sins have one common thread: they all want God to be dead and out of the picture. Each one shows how, with every fiber of our corrupted being, *we* want to be God. We want to do what we want to do when we want to do it. We wish to be the center of the universe. We want our will to be done. And we regard others not as gifts from the hand of a loving God, but as either objects for our use or potential rivals who pose a threat and must be subjugated to our will. Or, we are also pretty good at simply pretending we don't see others standing around us, in need. And this is the rebellion which God punishes in humanity time and again (temporal punishment) and that also deserves, even demands eternal punishment. This rebellion actually insists on receiving hell. "Go away, God, and leave me alone!" the sinful rebel screams. It actually asks for hell—being removed from God—foolishly imagining that it would be heaven.

So with the Church's public Confession of sins, there is no varnishing this. That is also why our public Confession does not list out individual sins as though they were the big deal. The big deal isn't what I've done or failed to do. The big deal is the sinner inside who wants God gone and me to take His place: the rebel whose rebellion takes the form of a myriad of sins, too numerous to list and which are never even able to be perceived entirely. "Who can discern his errors? Declare me innocent from hidden faults" (Psalm 19:12). It is Scripture that reveals that this rebellion against God brings me a sentence of death, a temporal and an eternal death. It is entirely just. In fact, it is what justice demands.

When we gather as the people of God, assembled in His presence, this Confession is usually the first order of business. Together, we own up to the truth about ourselves, brutal as it is. Depressing? Actually, not at all. Because there is a truth deeper than the one we speak about ourselves. It is the truth that God speaks to us about Himself and what He has done about the disaster inside each one of us. We call that truth the Absolution. It is when God justifies the sinner, declaring her or him to be righteous.

Let me be clear: the Absolution is not a gift we could ever give to ourselves. Self-absolution is no Absolution. Absolution always comes to us from outside, received as a gift and never as something we create and fashion for ourselves. Absolution is a startling, surprising gift. We own up to the truth of the verdict God's Law pronounces upon our very selves, our secret inner life, corrupted through and through, constantly breaking forth into external sins. We confess what we have deserved from Him because of this mess. We stand with Isaiah the prophet when the vision of the earthly temple gave way and he saw with his own eyes the holy, holy, holy One, praised by the fiery seraphim in endless song (see Isaiah 6). In terror we cry out, "Woe is me! I am undone!" and then in the moment of our despair, a messenger, an angel is sent with a burning coal from the very heart of the altar in God's temple. The angel touches us with the coal with the promise, "Behold, this has touched your lips; your guilt is taken away, and your sin atoned for" (Isaiah 6:7). In just the same way, in the Divine Service, God's messenger—our pastor—stands, turns toward us, and speaks words from the altar. That is, from the one final altar, from the cross. These are words burning with the fire of divine love:

Almighty God in His mercy has given His Son to die for you and for His sake forgives you all your sins. As a called and ordained servant of Christ, and by His authority, I therefore forgive you all your sins in the name of the Father and of the ✠ Son and of the Holy Spirit. (*LSB*, p. 151, 167)

In the mercy of almighty God, Jesus Christ was given to die for us, and for His sake God forgives us all our sins. To those who believe in Jesus Christ He gives the power to become the children of God and bestows on them the Holy Spirit. May the Lord, who has begun this good work in us, bring it to completion in the day of our Lord Jesus Christ. (*LSB*, p. 151, 167, 214)

Upon this your confession, I, by virtue of my office, as a called and ordained servant of the Word, announce the grace of God unto all of you, and in the stead and by the

command of my Lord Jesus Christ I forgive you all your sins in the name of the Father and of the ✠ Son and of the Holy Spirit. (*LSB*, p. 185)

The Absolution is not partial, not piecemeal; it is total. It is as sweeping in scope as the Confession that precedes it. All sins owned up to, and all sins absolved, forgiven, put under the blood of the Lamb of God. Not a single one left uncovered.

But can an Absolution be so broad and so certain in scope? Yes! It is grounded in two truths. First, the Absolution is solidly anchored in the universal atonement of our Savior, who by His blood has indeed won forgiveness for the entire world. The Absolution is one of the Lord's methods of delivering that universal forgiveness. "For all have sinned and fall short of the glory of God, and are justified by His grace as a gift, through the redemption that is in Christ Jesus, whom God put forward as a propitiation by His blood, to be received by faith" (Romans 3:23–25). "If we confess our sins, He is faithful and just to forgive us our sins and to cleanse us from all unrighteousness. . . . But if anyone does sin, we have an advocate with the Father, Jesus Christ the righteous. He is the propitiation for our sins, and not for ours only but also for the sins of the whole world" (1 John 1:9; 2:1–2). Second, the Absolution is the Blessed Trinity's forgiveness of a person. It is not so much something applied to sins as it is something applied to sinners. Notice this in Nathan's absolution of David in 2 Samuel 12:13: "The LORD also has put away your sin; *you* shall not die" (emphasis added). And in Jesus' absolution of the woman caught in the act of adultery in John 8:11: "Neither do I condemn *you*; go, and from now on sin no more" (emphasis added).

The Absolution, so sweeping in its nature, has sometimes troubled people. They wonder: "But what about the person who *isn't* sorry for their sins, has no terror at all, and walks away thinking: 'Cool! God likes to forgive; I like to sin. What a deal.'" In some times and places, Lutherans tried to deal with this misuse of the public Absolution by adding provisions into it. Here's an example from the sixteenth-century *Church Order for Braunschweig-Wolfenbüttel*:

> The Almighty God has had mercy on you and by the merit of the most holy suffering, death, and resurrection of His beloved Son, our Lord Jesus Christ, forgives you all your sins; and I, as an ordained minister of the Christian Church, announce to all who truly repent and who, by faith, place all their trust in the sole merit of Jesus Christ and who intend to conform their lives according to the command and will of God the forgiveness of all your sins, in the name of God the Father, the Son, and the Holy Spirit. Amen. But to all who are impenitent and unbelieving, I say, on the basis of God's Word and in the name of Jesus Christ, that God has retained your sins and will certainly punish them. (Martin Chemnitz, *Church Order*, trans. Jacob Corzine et al. [St. Louis: Concordia Publishing House, 2015], 85)

But here's the problem: many a person with a terrified conscience (like we described about Adam and Eve above) on hearing such an Absolution immediately makes the assumption that the Absolution really wasn't meant for them at all. That is why in our liturgical books we have kept to the other Lutheran tradition, from the revision of the liturgy in Saxony in the sixteenth century, of a free Absolution. The sermon is the place to make sure that the "impenitent and unbelieving" hear that they dare not appropriate to themselves the Absolution's comfort and joy; but the Absolution is offered in our liturgies in a form without provisions.

PRIVATE ABSOLUTION

A Christian goes faithfully to the Divine Service, makes Confession of sins, and hears the Absolution. Yet still sometimes in the middle of the night, he or she wakes up and remembers some sin committed. Perhaps it is a besetting sin, a characteristic weakness, something he or she struggles against time and time again and yet often falls into. It grieves this person and he or she wonders: "Can God really forgive me for that?" The poet John Donne captured this Christian struggle in his famous poem "A Hymn to God the Father." Consider these words:

Wilt thou forgive that sin where I begun,
  Which was my sin, though it were done before?
Wilt thou forgive that sin, through which I run,
  And do run still, though still I do deplore?
    When thou hast done, thou hast not done,
    For I have more.

Wilt thou forgive that sin which I have won
  Others to sin, and made my sin their door?
Wilt thou forgive that sin which I did shun
  A year or two, but wallow'd in, a score?
    When thou hast done, thou hast not done,
    For I have more.

I have a sin of fear, that when I have spun
  My last thread, I shall perish on the shore;
But swear by thyself, that at my death thy Son
  Shall shine as he shines now, and heretofore;
    And, having done that, thou hast done;
    I fear no more.

The Lord has an answer for this fear! It is the gift of the private Absolution. The Small Catechism describes it like this: "Before God we should plead guilty of all sins, even those we are not aware of, as we do in the Lord's Prayer; but before the pastor we should confess only those sins which we know and feel in our hearts" (Small Catechism, Confession, "What sins should we confess?"). When a particular sin is weighing down the heart, we come before the pastor and dare to name it. Why? So that we can receive the comfort that comes from the word of forgiveness targeted to the sinner who is troubled over specific sins. On page 292 in *Lutheran Service Book,* there is a service called "Individual Confession and Absolution."

Sadly, many Lutherans today have never experienced this private Absolution, which their ancestors in the faith treasured as such a great gift. This is such a shame! In fact, the Lutheran Confessions flat out assert that it would be wicked for the private Absolution to be taken out of the Church. Yes, we have been wicked. And the result is that we have left many Christians all alone to struggle with the sin in their lives, rather than bathing them in the comfort of personalized forgiveness addressed to them in their tangible struggles. Let's walk through the order of Individual Confession and Absolution to see what we have been missing out on.

The rubrics of this order are very important. First, we are invited to prepare ourselves by meditating on the Ten Commandments. These proclaim to us what holiness looks like, what the shape of love is to be in our lives. The more we ponder them, the more the Holy Spirit discloses the ways we have failed to love God above all and our neighbor as ourself. The point of this is not feeling miserable; the point is to force you to realize you can't fix yourself. It drives you to look outside yourself. The second rubric is also vital: if you are not

> THE CONFESSION, BECAUSE IT RESTS ON YOU, WILL NEVER BE PERFECT; THE ABSOLUTION, BECAUSE IT RESTS ON GOD'S PROMISE AND CHRIST'S SACRIFICE, ALWAYS IS!

burdened by particular sins, do not trouble yourself or search for or invent other sins, turning the gift into a torture! Rather, mention one or two sins that you know and let that be enough. The focus is on the Absolution, rather than Confession. The Confession, because it rests on you, will never be perfect; the Absolution, because it rests on God's promise and Christ's sacrifice, always is!

Unlike any other liturgy, this one does not start with the pastor talking. He is silent, waiting. When you have collected your thoughts and are ready, you kneel and say:

"Pastor, please hear my confession and pronounce forgiveness in order to fulfill God's will." (*LSB*, p. 292)

That's so beautiful right there. God's will is your forgiveness. God's will is that His forgiveness ring in your ear so that you believe and rejoice that the blood of His Son has answered for your every sin, with His perfect obedience even to the point of a bloody death on Golgotha. The pastor responds:

"Proceed."

The penitent (person confessing their sins) then continues:

"I, a poor sinner, plead guilty before God of all sins. I have lived as if God did not matter and as if I mattered most. My Lord's name I have not honored as I should; my worship and prayers have faltered. I have not let His love have its way with me, and so my love for others has failed. There are those whom I have hurt, and those whom I have failed to help. My thoughts and desires have been soiled with sin."

And here the penitent usually falters at least the first time. Speaking the generalities about sin as in the above Confession is painful, but what comes next is the hardest part: to name the sins that in fact trouble you.

"What troubles me particularly is that . . ."

There is no script at this point. Only the penitent can say what is eating at his or her heart and devouring his or her soul. The wise confessor (person hearing the confession) will allow for silence and have a box of tissues at hand. He never interrupts. This needs to be explained to the penitent beforehand. The pastor will only know that the confession has come to an end when the person concludes with the words:

"I am sorry for all of this and ask for grace. I want to do better."

That last bit is vital. The mark of an impenitent sinner is that they want what they imagine is forgiveness. That is, they want to be free from any negative consequences of their behaviors and attitudes, but they really do not want to be free of those behaviors or attitudes. The penitent sinner pleads for grace "to do better." Our theologians used to call this "the intention to amend one's sinful life" (see the Absolution from the church order cited above). In other words, it is the intention and desire to change. To be willing, by the grace of God, to actually live differently.

The pastor then gives a blessing:

"God be merciful to you and strengthen your faith."

"Amen."

Then a question is asked:

"Do you believe that my forgiveness is God's forgiveness?"

"Yes."

I once had a penitent stop at that point and ask me to explain that to him. I turned to John 20 and the words of Christ on the evening of His resurrection: "If you forgive anyone his sins, they are forgiven; if you do not forgive them, they are not forgiven" (Small Catechism, Confession, "Where is this written?", adapted from John 20:23). It is not the pastor's personal forgiveness. He is only the delivery man just as in the public Divine Service. He is forking over to the penitent what Christ has told him to give away to penitent sinners.

It is striking how this question is not the one that pietism expects. Not "Are you really and truly sorry that you have sinned?" The contrition is not explored. Once you have seen the mess and have begun to look outward, the answer is never to turn back toward your own heart; rather the answer is to turn to where God is standing ready to douse you in forgiveness. Rather than focusing on "being really sorry," faith is asked for. Do you believe?

The Absolution is short and to the point:

"Let it be done for you as you believe."

It also is pressed down upon the person's head, targeted by the laying on of hands:

The pastor places his hands on the head of the penitent and says:

"In the stead and by the command of my Lord Jesus Christ I forgive you all your sins in the name of the Father and of the ✠ Son and of the Holy Spirit."

"Amen."

The pastor will have listened carefully to the penitent's Confession—not to craft words of instruction about how to fix this or that sinful habit—but rather to know how to speak a personal word from the Scriptures to comfort the heart. I remember so well when I had made a confession to a pastor about the guilt of taking a call and moving many miles away from my mother when she was slipping toward advanced stages of Alzheimer's. The pastor concluded by setting before me Christ on the cross, taking care of His mother even in death. I remember the sinking feeling. Exactly. Exactly what I had not done. But ever so gently he said: "I say this to you not to give you an example, but to remind you that He has fulfilled the Fourth Commandment perfectly and He did that for you. That is your righteousness." Right after the Absolution, that was like another Absolution in itself, and it brought me such joy. It taught me as a pastor the importance of listening for how to comfort terrified sinners with specific accounts from the Scriptures that point to the perfect righteousness of Christ in a way that resonates with their experiences and their specific sins—the gift of Absolution.

Every pastor who is ordained in our church makes the promise never to divulge the sins confessed to him. Unfortunately, sometimes people believe that there are exceptions to this promise. It always is a wise thing to ask your pastor if he believes there are exceptions to this vow. If so, you should find a different confessor.

CONFESSION BETWEEN CHRISTIANS

Confessing sins publicly in the Divine Service (e.g., Corporate Confession and Absolution [LSB, pp. 290–291]) and privately with the pastor (e.g., Individual Confession and Absolution [LSB, pp. 292–293]) does not exhaust the role of confession in a Christian's life. We also are to confess our sins to one another, whenever we become aware that we have not loved our neighbor as God commands us to and that we have hurt others, particularly in words spoken or omitted, and in actions taken or neglected. God's great plan to destroy the evil one's power in our lives is to drown it in God's forgiveness. He wants this forgiveness to be on our lips constantly, flowing freely all the time and in all directions. So, if I was preoccupied and so spoke grumpily to my spouse in the morning, God gives me the gift of recollecting myself, turning to her before I head out to work, and saying: "That was uncalled for on my part. I am sorry. I shouldn't have spoken to you in that tone of voice. Will you forgive me?" Then God gives her the gift of saying: "Yes, in God's name, I forgive you. Be at peace." This constant humbling of ourselves as we stumble along in the Christian life together is the absolute key to genuinely Christian marriages, families, congregations, and friendships. We start all of these relationships knowing that we all are corrupted by original sin and confident that we will let each other down from time to time. But what holds us together as God's people is what never lets us down: forgiveness. Forgiveness asked and then imparted.

This is an area where we truly need a bit of work. We need to lose the noncommittal: "It's okay. Don't worry about it." We need to recover the full-blooded: "I forgive you. I forgive you in the name of Jesus, our great High Priest." None of us on our own has the capacity to forgive to the extent that others whom we love have the capacity to hurt and disappoint us. But in Jesus there is a fountain of forgiveness that is inexhaustible.

> WE NEED TO LOSE THE NONCOMMITTAL: "IT'S OKAY. DON'T WORRY ABOUT IT." WE NEED TO RECOVER THE FULL-BLOODED: "I FORGIVE YOU."

Remember how Peter wanted a reasonable limit: "Lord, how often will my brother sin against me, and I forgive him? As many as seven times?" Jesus blows the numbers away: "I do not say to you seven times, but seventy-seven times" (Matthew 18:21–22).

Peter was astounded, as are we. We don't have this capacity inside ourselves; we'd struggle to scrounge up the willingness to forgive the seven times. But Peter is asking this of the One who is the forgiveness of all of the sins of the whole world. In Him, we have come to a fountain of forgiveness that we cannot exhaust either for ourselves or for others. As we live in Him and His forgiveness, we set one another free constantly. This private use of the Office of the Keys is one of the great joys of recovered Christian piety. "Be kind to one another, tenderhearted, forgiving one another, as God in Christ forgave you" (Ephesians 4:32).

FOR DISCUSSION

1. What gives us the courage to speak the truth God's Word reveals about ourselves?

God's unshakeable love

2. What does God's Word show us about the depth of our sin?

Sinful & unclear p 18

3. What is the anchor, the Scriptural basis, for the Absolution?

Lord's way for universal forgiveness

4. When might a Christian seek out the gift of private Absolution and why is it such a blessing?

5. Why is confessing and being forgiven vital not only for our relationship with God but also for our relationships with others?

6. How is it possible to go on forgiving, no matter how much or how often?

forgive others as Christ forgives you.

CHAPTER 5

THE FIFTH GODLY HABIT:
Sacrificial Giving

The miracle of the feeding of the five thousand (plus!) is the only miracle of our Lord that appears in all four Gospels. Let's think about the account given in John 6:1–15. It is springtime, Passover time. Jesus is on a mountain with His disciples, and He has drawn a large crowd because of the "signs" He has been doing on the sick. "Sign" is the apostle John's favorite word for our Lord's miracles, hinting also that they point beyond themselves to something greater. As the crowd comes to Him, Jesus tosses a hot potato in Philip's lap: "Where are we to buy bread, so that these people may eat?" John lets us know that Jesus is testing Philip, since the Lord already knows exactly what He is going to do. Philip must have been "a numbers guy." He scans the crowd, estimates, and does the math. His assessment: the problem, the need is huge. He is crushed beneath the weight of it: "Two hundred denarii would not buy enough bread for each of them to get a little." That's like spending two-thirds of a year's income to solve a single meal problem! Philip stares into the crowd, paralyzed by the vastness of the problem.

Andrew comes along with help . . . sort of. He notes: "There is a boy here who has five barley loaves and two fish, but what are they for so many?" Was that the disciples' own dinner? Possibly. It seems about the right amount of food to feed the twelve disciples and Jesus.

Picture these two men: Philip, staring open mouthed at the crowd, overcome by the vastness of the need, while Andrew shakes his head over the meager resources in his hands. Do you see that both of them had their eyes trained on exactly the wrong spot? Both flunk the test that the Lord is giving. Both are trying to juggle the hot potato of the problem without getting burned; but they never seem to realize that the Lord tossed it to them, to train them to toss it back to Him, the One who could handle it.

Jesus has the people sit down, and He does verbs for the crowd that echo what he still does for us in the Eucharist: He takes the bread, gives thanks, and distributes. Same with the fish.

The image of the loaves and the fish was a popular drawing in the early Christian catacombs. Something about this miracle touches on the very heart of the Christian faith.

From the parallel accounts, it becomes clear that the disciples actually do the distributing (see Matthew 14:19; Mark 6:41; Luke 9:16). If they are handing out their own dinner, as some have suggested, this gets even more interesting. Jesus, in effect, says: "Here, go, give it away!" Can you see Peter gulp as he looks from the little bit of bread in his hand to the group seated in the grass? Can you see him break off a measly piece, trying to make it stretch. And when did it dawn on them? When did they see that no matter how much they broke off and gave away, the lump in their hand remained the same? Can you see the astonishment on their faces as they look back to Him? Was He smiling? And then they began their work in earnest, without fear now. I imagine even with laughter! "My thoughts are not your thoughts, neither are your ways My ways, declares the LORD" (Isaiah 55:8).

But let's not rush past an important point here. Stop and ask yourself: what would have happened if the disciples had held onto their little lunch, had kept it for themselves in fear, terrified that there would be no more if they gave it away and that they would go hungry? How much would each have had at the close of that day? A handful! That's it. But Jesus began to open their eyes that day to see a new truth in God's economy. By giving away to others, they ended up richer themselves! They ended up with a basket of bread each, far more than that fistful they had started out with. Hands clenching in fear were transformed into hands opened wide to give away.

Six chapters later in John, Jesus opens up the deeper meaning of this sign to the disciples and to us. Not by accident, it is again Philip and Andrew who are involved. Philip is approached by some Greeks at the feast (another Passover feast, the last in Jesus' ministry) who ask to see Jesus, to meet the mighty miracle worker. Philip brings their request to Andrew, and together the two disciples lay the matter before Jesus. Hear Jesus' curious response: "The hour has come for the Son of Man to be glorified. Truly, truly I say to you, unless a grain of wheat falls into the earth and dies, it remains alone; but if it dies, it bears much fruit. Whoever loves his life loses it, and whoever hates his life in this world will keep it for eternal life" (John 12:23–25).

You can eat grain; just as the disciples could have eaten the bread from the small boy that day in Galilee. But then it is gone. It nourishes you once. Or you can do what surely looks like folly: you can lose your food—give it away; plant it; let it fall into the earth and die. The reality, of course, is that our farmers and gardeners do this all the time. You plant what you could have eaten and out from the planted seed, which seems dead and lost to us, comes up a crop. Some thirtyfold, some sixtyfold, and some a hundredfold (cf. Mark 4:8). This unlocks for us one of the truly amazing principles of the Kingdom. It is not at variance with nature, but rather it is at variance with fallen man's warped perception and fears! The principle is you gain more by giving away rather than by holding on. That is what Jesus proclaimed to Philip and Andrew when the Greeks asked to see Jesus. The pre-eminent proof of this "giving away to receive," "losing life to find," was how our Lord gave Himself up on the Cross. He was just like the grain of wheat, falling into the ground, and so losing His life. And yet the loss of His life brought in a bumper crop of new lives: He rose from the dead as "the firstborn among many brothers" (Romans 8:29) and "the firstfruits of those who have fallen asleep" (1 Corinthians 15:20).

You might be wondering, "What on earth does all this have to do with a chapter on sacrificial giving?" Absolutely everything! What hinders our giving? Is it not fear? We hold tightly to our stuff and our money because we are afraid that the stuff we have accumulated may not be enough. True riches come from recognizing that every last thing we "possess" (a misnomer if there ever was one) is in point of fact solely a gift from the Father in heaven. And He has more to give than we will ever need. Everything you call your own comes from the God who loves you, who will not fail to give you your daily bread, and who will do so solely out of His own goodness and mercy, without any merit or worthiness in you. He does it out of love.

The catechism drives this truth home to us with the verbs in the explanation of the First Article of the Apostles' Creed:

I believe in God, the Father Almighty, Maker of heaven and earth.

What does this mean?

I believe that God has MADE me and all creatures; that He has GIVEN me my body and soul, eyes, ears, and all my members, my reason and all my senses, and still TAKES CARE of them. He also GIVES me clothing and shoes, food and drink, house and home, wife and children, land, animals, and all I have. He richly and daily PROVIDES me with all that I need to support this body and life. He defends me against all danger and guards and protects me from all evil. All this He does only out of fatherly, divine goodness and mercy, without any merit or worthiness in me. For all this it is my duty to thank and praise, serve and obey Him.

This is most certainly true. (emphasis added)

You have a Father! Fathers provide for their children. Your Father has given you, first of all, your very self. His giving doesn't stop there, though. He also gives you clothing, food, shelter, family—in fact, everything you have. And He promises that He will *richly and daily* provide you with all that you will ever need to support your body and life. Fear—which leads to stinginess in giving—is always, at root, forgetting and doubting the Father's love.

Do you remember what happened when the Israelites, wandering in the wilderness, were afraid there might not be manna tomorrow? They hadn't been following the Lord for very long, and they didn't understand His ways yet. In fear that He might somehow let them down and not provide for them, some of them tried to store up extra manna for the next day. They soon learned that that didn't work. The stored-up manna instantly rotted, stank, and bred worms. The stench went deeper than rotting food, however; it was also the stench of not trusting that the heavenly Father will provide what His children need.

When Jesus fed the five thousand, He took bread and "looked up to heaven" (Luke 9:16). By that simple action, He reminded

> WHEN JESUS FED THE FIVE THOUSAND, HE TOOK BREAD AND "LOOKED UP TO HEAVEN" HE REMINDED THE DISCIPLES AND US TO LOOK. NOT AT THE LITTLENESS OF WHAT WE MIGHT HAVE IN HAND. NOT AT THE VASTNESS OF THE NEED. NOT AT OUR OWN INADEQUACIES AND FEARS. RATHER, LOOK TO THE FATHER.

the disciples and us *where* to look. Not at the littleness of what we might have in hand. Not at the vastness of the need. Not at our own inadequacies and fears. Rather, look to the Father. James wrote: "Every good gift and every perfect gift is from above, coming down from the Father of lights, with whom there is no variation or shadow due to change" (James 1:17). Look to the One who did not fail to provide us with the gift of His Son, our Bridegroom. St. Paul cries out in astonishment, "He who did not spare His own Son but gave Him up for us all, how will He not also with Him graciously give us all things?" (Romans 8:32). The One who gave you Jesus will not fail to meet your bodily needs. He loves you, and so He provides every day whatever you need to support your body and life. This truly frees our hands from clutching to our money and our stuff. When your Father owns everything in the entire universe and has given you an infallible proof of His love for you by giving His Son up for you on a cross, you can be like Abraham and say: "The LORD will provide" (Genesis 22:14).

God wants to free us from clutching to what we have in fear because, put most simply, God wants us to know the joy of giving. I don't think anyone ever captured this so beautifully as St. Francis did in his famous prayer:

> **O divine Master, grant that I may not so much seek**
> **to be consoled as to console,**
> **to be understood as to understand,**
> **to be loved as to love.**
> **For it is *in giving that we receive*,**
> **it is in pardoning that we are pardoned,**
> **and it is in dying that we are born to eternal life.**[5]

---

5. "Peace Prayer of Saint Francis," Loyola Press, accessed September 6, 2017, https://www.loyolapress .com/our-catholic-faith/prayer/traditional-catholic-prayers/saints-prayers/peace-prayer-of-saint-francis (emphasis added).

It is in giving that one receives. I doubt that there is a single one of you reading these words who hasn't tasted that truth at some point in your life. A time when you were enriched and felt joyous and free after encountering a need and simply meeting it in love.

So, giving is the key, yes, but also *sacrificial* giving. What does that mean? Jesus pointed to a widow putting her mite, her two small copper coins, into the temple collection. He said a surprising thing about her: she gave *more* than all of the other people, even those who were pouring the big bucks into the offering box and doing so with great ostentation. Why? "They all contributed out of their abundance, but she out of her poverty put in all she had to live on" (Luke 21:4). To put it simply, her total giving witnessed to her total faith in the heavenly Father and his ability and desire to care for her. She was so free because of her total trust in God's provision that she could joyfully contribute everything she had. She quite literally was giving herself in that gift. The rich gave abundantly, but their giving didn't really cost them that much, and therefore, it didn't give evidence of any great trust in the Father. They still had plenty left over for themselves. They knew where their next meal was coming from; she didn't—except she knew that her heavenly Father would take care of her.

Such sacrificial giving causes something inside of you to die. What dies is the impulse to fret about not having enough, the unbelief that would tie love's hands in fear. That is the thing that is sacrificed in every act of sacrificial giving, each time teaching us to lift our eyes to the heavenly Father and remember with joy who He is and who we are.

But we must also beware of a mechanical sort of giving that can creep into even the greatest sacrifices in our lives and rob them of their true joy. St. Paul expresses this in his famous chapter on love or charity: "If I give away all I have, and if I deliver up my body to be burned, but have not love, I gain nothing" (1 Corinthians 13:3). I believe that this is the key to what our Lord was intending in that mysterious statement recorded in Luke, "But give as alms those things that are within, and behold, everything is clean for you" (Luke 11:41). What does it mean for alms to remain external? What does it mean for alms to be from within?

If you've ever ridden a subway in one of our major cities, you might have received the advice: "Never look them in the eye." The "them" are the many beggars you encounter in any urban center. The whole idea is if you don't look the beggar in the eye, you avoid acknowledging him or her as a *person*. For if you do acknowledge that the beggar is a person, then the gig is up. Then you have to face the fact that this is a human being made in the image and likeness of God, called just like you and me to be a child of the heavenly Father. I heard an interview on Tim Ferris's podcast a few months ago that helped with this enormously. The famous psychologist Dr. Phil Zimbardo warns against speaking of "the homeless" or "the immigrants." Rather, they are *persons* without homes; *persons* who have had to leave their homeland. When he gives a gift to a homeless *person* begging on the street, he stops, introduces himself, and asks the person's name. Then he tells the person he wishes he had more to give, gives his gift, and wishes them well. This is alms *from within*; such encounters acknowledge the inherent dignity and value of the person before us, their worth as a creation of God, and so also their worth as our very own brother or sister.

How utterly transformed our almsgiving would be if we remembered that each encounter with a human need is an opportunity and a gift actually to us. Each encounter is an opportunity to be called out from our inner world and our preoccupation with ourselves. We are invited to move into the world and sphere of another person's needs, to welcome their presence in our lives as a gift from the heavenly Father (whether the person knows that or not), and to be a blessing to that person, as Christ has been a blessing to both of us. St. Paul in Acts cites a saying of Jesus that does not appear in the canonical Gospels but which rings true with everything Jesus ever taught: "It is more blessed to give than to receive" (Acts 20:35).

Sacrificial giving, giving alms from within, actually in the end is one of the greatest joys of life. Not the sort of giving that says, "Look at me! Look how much I am contributing! How much I must love!" Rather, it is the sort of giving that forgets about the self because it is solidly attuned to the person in need before us.

God's delight in that kind of giving is shown throughout the pages of Scripture: "Blessed is the man who fears the LORD, who greatly delights in His commandments! . . . His heart is firm, trusting in the LORD. His heart is steady; he will not be afraid, until he looks in triumph on his adversaries. He has distributed freely; he has given to the poor; his righteousness endures forever" (Psalm 112:1, 7–9). "Whoever is generous to the poor lends to the LORD, and He will repay him for his deed" (Proverbs 19:17). "And [the angel] said: 'Cornelius, your prayer has been heard and your alms have been remembered before God'" (Acts 10:31).

Alms giving to those who are poor, is not the only form of sacrificial giving in the life of the Christian. There is also the regular support of the Church's ministry and mission. Here, the Old Testament has some intriguing light to shed. We see before the Mosaic Law was ever given, people responded to encounters with the Lord's gracious gifts by giving the tithe, the tenth part. We first encounter this in Abram in Genesis 14 and the mysterious meeting with Melchizedek. God had granted a deliverance and rescue of Lot and his company through Abram. As Abram came back from this, he met Melchizedek, the King of Salem, said to be priest of God Most High; Melchizedek brought forth bread and wine and blessed Abram. In response, "Abram gave him a tenth of everything" (Genesis 14:20).

Similarly, Abram's grandson Jacob had a vision at Bethel (see Genesis 28:10–22) in which God promised to be with him, bless him, and bring him back safely to the land of promise. Perhaps thinking of how God had done each of these things for his grandfather Abraham, Jacob promised, "Of all that You give me, I will give a full tenth to You"

(Genesis 28:22). The tithe, then, seems to have originally grown out of joyous gratitude in response to a surprise blessing from God. Herein lies the key: the tithe in the Old Testament first and foremost confessed that God is the Giver of all. It is only giving back to Him what is His. Truly, as David confessed in 1 Chronicles 29:14: "But who am I, and what is my people, that we should be able thus to offer willingly? For all things come from You, and of Your own we have given You." We sing the same thought in this famous hymn:

> We give Thee but Thine own,
> Whate'er the gift may be;
> All that we have is Thine alone,
> A trust, O Lord, from Thee.
>
> May we Thy bounties thus
> As stewards true receive
> And gladly, as Thou blessest us,
> To Thee our firstfruits give!
>
> —*LSB* 781:1–2

In the Mosaic Law, the tithe became a statute for the people of Israel. We see how seriously God took this in Malachi 3:6–12 where God charged the children of Jacob with breaking the Seventh Commandment, robbing Him, stealing from Him, "in your tithes and contributions" (Malachi 3:8). It is true, of course, that "the earth is the Lord's and the fullness thereof" (Psalm 24:1), and therefore He needs nothing from us. But the particular way Israel was supposed to confess this was to offer back to the bountiful Giver the tenth part. Our Lord excoriated the scribes and Pharisees for their scrupulosity in tithing even their tiny seeds (mint, dill, cumin) while neglecting the weightier matters of the law: justice and mercy and faithfulness. Yet, He does not condemn tithing, but rather He says, "These you ought to have done, without neglecting the others" (Matthew 23:23).

It is true, of course, that the Christian is no more bound by the Mosaic Law of the tithe than he is by the command to circumcise on the eighth day. In its strict sense, the tithe is a ceremonial law that is no longer binding on anyone who has been baptized into Christ. However, the impulse to tithe as a joyous response to the Creator's bountiful gifts remains, just as the pattern of this response preceded the Mosaic Law. This spontaneous giving as love's response to the Creator and therefore to sisters and brothers in need is what we see Paul describe in the great "stewardship" chapters of 2 Corinthians 8 and 9. Consider:

> *"For in a severe test of affliction, their abundance of joy and their extreme poverty have overflowed in a wealth of generosity on their part. For they gave according to their means, as I can testify, and beyond their means, of their own free will, begging us earnestly for the favor of taking part in the relief of the saints—and this, not as we expected, but they gave themselves first to the Lord and then by the will of God to us."* (*2 Corinthians 8:2–5*)

> *"For if the readiness is there, it is acceptable according to what a person has, not according to what he does not have."* (*2 Corinthians 8:12*)

> *"Each one must give as he has made up in his mind, not reluctantly or under compulsion, for God loves a cheerful giver."* (*2 Corinthians 9:7*)

So, many Christians across the years, completely free in Christ, have taken as a template for their giving to the Church Abram and Jacob's spontaneous offerings of the tithe. The tenth of what they receive they give to God as a confession that it all comes from Him and because they desire to be partners in the sharing of the Gospel (see Philippians 1:3–5; 4:14–16). Their giving is called forth by love for others and animated from within by the joy of the Cheerful Giver, God Himself. This joyful and loving giving is directed to the support of the Church's ministry and mission precisely because Christians believe sharing the love of God in Christ with another person is the best way we can love them and the only way they can come to know true joy.

In the New Testament, the tithe is a godly pattern for supporting the Church's ministry and the spread of the Good News; but it is not something that can ever be commanded by one person to another. Giving under compulsion would be giving without love (which, if you recall, Paul pointed out is useless in 1 Corinthians 13), and it would be giving without joy. However, on the other hand, the Christian ought to never treat the tithe as the extent or limit of his or her giving. The tithe is not a tax like when you give to the government (grudgingly, all too often) what it says you owe, and then you wouldn't think about giving it one penny more. Instead, because giving is an opportunity for joy, we do not measure it by "have to" but "get to." After all, we are only giving to the Church of the Father's bounty. And there is no end to that. The Spirit who enlivens Christian giving opens eyes to see not only that the Father's bounty can never be exhausted, but that part of the unique gift that God wants to give the human person is to share in His joy in giving. That giving is itself a path and entrance into joy.

Generosity is a vital aspect of how God enlivens us. He has no life to share with us but His own eternal life. That life is at its core a life of giving, of pouring out Himself for us with His gifts. Listen to Luther on this in the Large Catechism:

In it we see how the Father has given Himself to us together with everything of His making and how He most richly provides for us in this life, quite apart from all the other inexpressible eternal blessings showered on us through His Son and His Holy Spirit. (Janzow 70)

For in these three articles [of the Creed] God Himself has revealed and disclosed the deepest profundity of His fatherly heart, His sheer inexpressible love. He created us for the very purpose that He might redeem us and make us holy. And besides giving and entrusting to us everything in heaven and on earth, He has given us His Son and His Holy Spirit in order to bring us to Himself through them. (Janzow 77)

For He is an eternally unchangeable fountain which, the more it gushes forth and overflows, the more it gives of itself. (Janzow 87)

God's very being is giving. The Father gives Himself entirely to the Son, and the Son in the Holy Spirit gives Himself entirely to the Father: and the Father creates us so that He gives Himself through His Son and Spirit entirely to us.

This giving of self, not just of things but of presents in the true meaning of that word—a gift which carries presence—is what carries hristian along in a current of giving—or one might even call it estyle of giving." The need of my neighbor becomes to me a gift n God, an opportunity to grow in the grace of giving. We come to taste personally the truth of the Lord Jesus' words that it is more blessed to give than to receive. As we pointed out above, this is not just in relation to money, but also to our time and our attention—something which is a rare gift in these days, distracted as we are by our many electronic gadgets!

The sacrificial nature of this giving means that something of ourself has gone into the gift. My sister-in-law has a loom set up in her family room. She weaves the most wonderful blankets. She has given a baby blanket to each of my grandchildren. Something of Aunt Debbi comes with each gift. The same is true of the blankets and hats my wife has crocheted over the years and given away. It wasn't just a "thing"; for by her labor, my wife became a part of the gift. The same is true of a meal you sweat over in the kitchen, pack up, and carry to a neighbor in need. Or of an hour or two you spend cleaning the gutters and raking the leaves for an elderly widow who is trying desperately to continue living in her home. Christian giving is so much more than money; the tithe, then, is really just practice for and a reflection of a whole life offered back as a living sacrifice to the God who gave us everything: "I appeal to you, therefore, brothers, by the mercies of God, to present your bodies as a living sacrifice, holy and acceptable to God, which is your spiritual worship" (Romans 12:1).

FOR DISCUSSION

1. What important truth did our Lord teach Philip and Andrew in John 6?

Toss problems back to God.

2. How was that a sign of a deeper truth He taught in John 12?

you gain more by giving away.

3. What frees the Christian to give?

give away to receive

4. What does it mean to give "alms from within"?

5. In addition to alms to the poor, why do Christians delight in the habit of giving to the Church?

6. What role can the tithe play in Christian giving?

Support missionary

7. How does the joy of giving spill over into many areas of our lives?

giving is a path + entrance into joy

CHAPTER 6

THE SIXTH GODLY HABIT:
Confessing Christ

There has been a sad tendency to beat Christians over the head for not sharing Christ with non-Christians as they ought. I doubt there is a single Christian who hasn't felt more than a twinge of guilt about not talking about Jesus more readily with others. What is the cause of the wimpy witness? Is it a problem of technique? Do we need to discover some better method for sharing the Gospel?

There was a time, not too many years ago, when we Lutherans tried to promote a basic outline that could do that job. But there was a problem. That approach came across to many of those to whom we witnessed—and many of us as well—as though we were doing a canned data dump, just sharing information, without actually interacting with the person before us. It appeared as though we engaged with them with ulterior motives: not because we were genuinely interested in them, but because we wished to impart data to them and wanted to manipulate the situation so that they would be receptive to what we wanted to share—a bait and switch tactic. For us, it made sharing the precious Gospel like peddling a commodity, maybe a vacuum cleaner or a set of encyclopedias, even if it was a commodity we were angling to give away for free! But that's not how we operate in other areas of life.

> THAT'S NOT HOW WE OPERATE IN OTHER AREAS OF LIFE.

I just finished reading a very good book on theology that challenged me with its fresh insights in the Scriptures and the authentic way those insights rang true. So what did I do? Keep this to myself? I couldn't. I wouldn't. There was no guilt driving me: "Weedon, you should be sharing this." Instead, what drove me to share it was my enjoyment, my delight, and my surprise in the book. So I said to my friend, Kevin, "Dude, you HAVE to read this book! I mean, it will blow you away! Check it out!" And I shared a bit or two from it to whet his appetite.

When we think about other parts of our lives, we realize we instinctively praise to others what we ourselves enjoy. Part of finding delight in something, the finishing touch of delighting in something, in fact, is praising it to others. We do this with people we enjoy talking with and being with because we want them to enjoy it as well; we love our friends and our family, and we want them to enjoy something that we think is good. We do this all the time. We do it with books, beautiful vistas, good restaurants, new diets, music, recipes, you name it!

> WHEN WE THINK ABOUT OTHER PARTS OF OUR LIVES, WE REALIZE WE INSTINCTIVELY PRAISE TO OTHERS WHAT WE OURSELVES ENJOY.

Are you starting to see how this relates to sharing Jesus with other people? Listen to the psalmist: "Oh, magnify the LORD with me, and let us exalt His name together! . . . Oh, taste and see that the LORD is good! Blessed is the man who takes refuge in Him!" (Psalm 34:3, 8). The psalmist urges us to taste the goodness of the Lord and then join him in speaking and singing God's praise. Does that sound like an odd way of speaking: to "taste" God's goodness? Actually it shouldn't. For us New Testament Christians, the image seems to fit rather well, actually, when we think about the Eucharist! The one who has tasted the joys of trusting in the Lord and experienced for himself how good it is, like when one has tasted good food, simply cannot refrain from urging others to enjoy tasting this goodness too: the goodness of trusting in the Lord.

Think of how chapter 1 of John's Gospel reflects this. John the Baptist witnessed to Jesus: "Behold, the Lamb of God!" Two of John's disciples heard John and began following Jesus. Jesus noticed He was being tracked and turned to ask them: "What are you seeking?" They asked Him: "Rabbi, where are You staying?" He invited them to come and see. They spent the rest of the day with Him. Then Andrew, one of the two, went and found his brother Peter. Andrew said, "We have found the Messiah" and brought Peter along to meet Jesus. Philip found his friend Nathanael and said to him, "We have found Him of whom Moses in the Law and also the prophets wrote, Jesus of Nazareth, the son of Joseph." Nathanael was skeptical that Nazareth could produce anyone of significance, let alone the Messiah. But Philip responded with a move from Jesus' playbook. He countered Nathanael's skepticism not with an argument, but an invitation: "Come and see." Nathanael took him up on the invitation, encountered Jesus, and walked away confessing, "Rabbi, You are the Son of God! You are the King of Israel!" (John 1:29–51).

"Come and see"! This is the heart of the Church's witness. A gracious and unexpected invitation for people to check out Jesus for themselves. One of the best case studies for this is in John 4. There, we see a pattern for inviting people to meet Jesus by how Jesus Himself interacts with a Samaritan woman. And there we realize the reason we invite people to meet Jesus is because the Father's mission is seeking those who worship Him in Spirit and in truth. The story takes place when Jesus' disciples have gone into the village to find food, and Jesus is alone beside the Sychar well in Samaria. A woman comes from the town. It is noon—not the usual time to be fetching water. Some have supposed she came there at that time because she was a bit of a *persona non grata* among the other women of the village. She pointedly ignores Jesus (obviously a Jew) and sets about her chore when suddenly His voice rings out: "Give me a drink." She apparently is quite shocked that a Jewish man would ask anything of her, "a woman of Samaria." But then He extends the invitation even further: "If you knew the gift of God, and who it is that is saying to you, 'Give me a drink,' you would have asked Him, and He would have given you living water" (John 4:10). The gift of God, of course, is the Son Himself, who came to be the Bridegroom of God's people. This woman has been aching for the sort of love THIS Bridegroom could give without ever realizing it. Yet here He is now: He has come into the flesh to give her living water—an image for the Holy Spirit who is Love as a Person. Characteristic of John's discourses, though, she misunderstands what Jesus means. She notes that He has nothing to draw with and the well is deep. "Where do You get that living water? Are You greater than our father Jacob?" (John 4:11–12).

Since she doesn't understand His invitation yet, He says more: "Everyone who drinks of this water will be thirsty again, but whoever drinks of the water that I will give him will never be thirsty forever. The water that I will give him will become in him a spring of water welling up to eternal life" (4:13–14). She is intrigued, but still misses the point. She likes the idea of not having to come here so often, so she asks Jesus for this gift He is talking about, "Sir, give me this water, so that I will not be thirsty or have to come here to draw water" (4:15).

How will He give her the living water? He has her interest now, having intrigued her by kindly regarding her and promising her great things. Now He needs to show her the greatness of the gift; so He says, "Go, call your husband, and come here" (4:16). She prevaricates, "I have no husband" (4:17). He agrees, "You are right in saying, 'I have no husband'; for you have had five husbands, and the one you now have is not your husband. What you have said is true."

Jesus exposes the wound in her heart. "Looking for love in all the wrong places," as the song says. She has gone through one man after another and yet never found the love that her heart aches for. And the sorrows have only mounted up. "But how on earth does this man know all this?" she must be thinking.

Being exposed is a crucial part of a person's encounter with Jesus. He has a way that opens up the human heart and sees it for what it is. "All are naked and exposed to the eyes of Him to whom we must give account" (Hebrews 4:13). This is the experience St. Paul describes as happening in worship services in 1 Corinthians: "But if all prophesy, and an unbeliever or outsider enters, he is convicted by all, he is called to account by all, *the secrets of his heart are disclosed*, and so, falling on his face, he will worship God and declare that God is really among you" (1 Corinthians 14:24–25, emphasis added). This is not an exposure that is accomplished by the proverbial hellfire and brimstone preaching or by yelling and shouting dire threats. It is accomplished with the tenderness with which Jesus is dealing with the woman at the Sychar well. We recall how in the previous chapter of John's Gospel Jesus stressed that He had not come to condemn the world, but to save it. He is not out to send anyone to hell; He has come instead to "[open] the kingdom of heaven to all believers" (Te Deum). What is crucial is that truth is spoken which brings to light the wound in the human heart: its utter failure in loving and finding love.

But the truth can be very painful to face. Jesus exposes the wound in the Samaritan woman's heart, but she would rather change the subject. She concedes, "Sir, I perceive that You are a prophet. Our fathers worshiped on this mountain, but you say that in Jerusalem is the place where people ought to worship" (John 4:19–20). This was not the first or last time theology was used to try to dodge the penetrating eyes of the Lord. Jesus is gentle with her even still; and yet He also uses her diversion to direct her where He wants her to go. "Woman, believe Me, the hour is coming when neither on this mountain nor in Jerusalem will you worship the Father. You worship what you do not know; we worship what we know, for salvation is from the Jews. But the hour is coming, and is now here, when the true worshipers will worship the Father in spirit and truth, for the Father is seeking such people to worship Him. God is spirit, and those who worship Him must worship in spirit and in truth" (John 4:21–24).

Jesus is changing her conception of who God is and how He relates to her. What He is describing is the triune God's mission: the Father sends the Son who accomplishes our salvation and sends the Holy Spirit; the Holy Spirit's great task is to take idol worshipers and transform them into worshipers of the Trinity. His work is to bring people to the Son in faith that the Son may present them to the Father. This is the worship in Spirit and in Truth that the Father seeks: He seeks those to whom He can give His gifts through His Spirit and His Son, who is the Truth (cf. John 1:14; 14:6).

She is beginning to understand what is happening in this conversation. She says what she understands: "I know that Messiah is coming (He who is called Christ). When He comes, He will tell us all things" (John 4:25). It seems Jesus' uncanny knowledge of her past recalls for her what she had been taught about the Messiah unlocking the mysteries of life. Jesus then tells her plainly what she is hinting at: "I who speak to you am He" (4:26).

At this moment, the disciples return. They are astonished to see Jesus talking with a Samaritan woman. None of them asks, "What are You seeking through this conversation, Jesus?" But if they had, they would have found out: "I seek this woman, just as I seek you. My Father sent Me here to seek and to save the lost."

John never misses a detail, and they all are important to helping us understand the story. The woman leaves her water jar when she runs away to tell the people in the town about Jesus. Get it? She now has the living water! She shouts in the middle of the town for anyone to hear: "Come, see a man who told me all that I ever did. Can this be the Christ?" (John 4:29). She is speaking an invitation as one who has had a surprise encounter with Jesus—an encounter in which He exposed the wounds of her heart, and yet He did not condemn her. Instead,

He loved her, spoke kindly to her, accepted her, and invited her into the true worship of His Father, a true relationship with His Father.

You can imagine some of the townsfolk snorting, "He told you 'all you ever did.' That must have been some story, given your history." Nevertheless, there is something in the way she witnesses to her encounter with Jesus that they find compelling. They must be able to see that this encounter has changed her. Being invited by the heavenly Bridegroom will do that. So they go with her to check it out for themselves; Jesus is watching and waiting for them. As the people begin to gather, Jesus cries out to His disciples, "Look, I tell you, lift up your eyes, and see that the fields are white for harvest."

We wish that the evangelist had given more information about Jesus' conversations with the townsfolk, but all we know is that after a several-day encounter with Jesus, the people tell the original woman, "It is no longer because of what you said that we believe, for we have heard for ourselves, and we know that this is indeed the Savior of the world" (John 4:41). The fields were indeed ripe for harvest.

So, in summary: one person encounters the Lord Jesus; her wonder and curiosity are stirred as He says He brings the gifts of God; she comes to realize that He is the Gift of God, the Messiah, who reveals all things when He exposes the wounds of the heart; and yet He is so gentle with her she wants to run and tell everyone she knows to come meet Him too: "Come, see a man who told me all I ever did. Could this be the Christ?" So the ones who are invited come, and they "see this man"—they meet Him, hear Him, and they come to believe that He is the Savior. To their great astonishment.

This pattern is just the same with us. When we encounter Jesus, He leaves us in awe and wonder. He sees us as we are, and yet He tenderly and lovingly forgives us and heals us. Out of us arises a spontaneous, "Come!" wanting everyone we know to also have this experience. "Come!" we say. "This is amazing; it will blow your mind. You have got to come and check this out!" As we said at the start of this chapter, we naturally praise to others what we ourselves have tasted and enjoyed. Our enjoyment of something is never complete until we turn to another and say: "How awesome is that?" Isn't that why when we're alone and something impresses us, we're inclined immediately to grab our phones and snap a picture? We want to share with others what we have enjoyed and invite them to enter into the joy it has given us.

If we think about this and our "witnessing crisis," we should immediately be able to go to the heart of the problem. Our witness falters when we ourselves have not enjoyed the surprise gift that is our Lord Jesus Christ in His community, the Church. Has attending church become a "have to" for you? Or is worship the place where Jesus constantly astounds you—His words exposing the secrets of your heart and His promises bathing you in a love that is "unasked, unforced, unearned" (to quote Jaroslav Vajda, *LSB* 369:4)? What a pure and astounding gift the Divine Service is.

> OUR WITNESS FALTERS WHEN WE OURSELVES HAVE NOT ENJOYED THE SURPRISE GIFT THAT IS OUR LORD JESUS CHRIST IN HIS COMMUNITY, THE CHURCH.

In the Divine Service, Jesus comes in His words to serve you. When you reflect on how the Divine Service is all about Jesus wanting to serve you and choosing to serve you when He could do anything but that, you can't help exclaiming how amazing this is to others. In fact, we even begin doing this in the course of the service itself.

Have you ever thought of the great connection between hymnody and witness? Note in particular that many hymns are not first addressed to God; they are addressed to each other concerning God's great works. In the New Testament, the Christian community was even exhorted to "[address] one another in psalms and hymns and spiritual songs, singing and making melody to the Lord with all your heart" (Ephesians 5:19).

When we praise God and make our melody to the Lord, we are also exhorting each other to enjoy Him and to trust Him; we are proclaiming with gladness the great things He has done. Luther has a classic hymn on this: "Dear Christians, One and All Rejoice!" Read these words and see how they invite and urge us all to taste the goodness of the Lord in His surprising deeds for us:

Dear Christians, one and all, rejoice,
　With exultation springing,
And with united heart and voice
　And holy rapture singing,
Proclaim the wonders God has done,
How His right arm the vict'ry won.
　What price our ransom cost Him!

Fast bound in Satan's chains I lay;
　Death brooded darkly o'er me.
Sin was my torment night and day;
　In sin my mother bore me.
But daily deeper still I fell;
My life became a living hell,
　So firmly sin possessed me.

My own good works all came to naught,
　No grace or merit gaining;
Free will against God's judgment fought,
　Dead to all good remaining.
My fears increased till sheer despair
Left only death to be my share;
　The pangs of hell I suffered.

But God had seen my wretched state
Before the world's foundation,

And mindful of His mercies great,
He planned for my salvation.
He turned to me a father's heart;
He did not choose the easy part
But gave His dearest treasure.

God said to His belovèd Son:
"It's time to have compassion.
Then go, bright jewel of My crown,
And bring to all salvation.
From sin and sorrow set them free;
Slay bitter death for them that they
May live with You forever."

The Son obeyed His Father's will,
Was born of virgin mother;
And God's good pleasure to fulfill,
He came to be my brother.
His royal pow'r disguised He bore;
A servant's form, like mine, He wore
To lead the devil captive.

To me He said: "Stay close to Me,
I am your rock and castle.
Your ransom I Myself will be;
For you I strive and wrestle.

For I am yours, and you are Mine,
And where I am you may remain;
  The foe shall not divide us.

"Though he will shed My precious blood,
  Me of My life bereaving,
All this I suffer for your good;
  Be steadfast and believing.
Life will from death the vict'ry win;
My innocence shall bear your sin,
  And you are blest forever.

"Now to My Father I depart,
  From earth to heav'n ascending,
And, heavn'ly wisdom to impart,
  The Holy Spirit sending;
In trouble He will comfort you
And teach you always to be true
  And into truth shall guide you.

"What I on earth have done and taught
  Guide all your life and teaching;
So shall the kingdom's work be wrought
  And honored in your preaching.
But watch lest foes with base alloy
The heav'nly treasure should destroy;
  This final word I leave you."

—*LSB 556*

I know lots of people love the hymn "I Love to Tell the Story." But, ironically, that hymn doesn't actually tell the story.[6] Speaking about the Gospel is not speaking the Gospel. Note how Luther's hymn, in contrast, does tell the Good News, and note how it tells it. The Gospel comes as a surprise joy that the singer invites all Christians to savor again so freshly that they quite literally jump for joy ("springing"!).

Another from Luther's pen that does a quite similar job is a paraphrase of the Creed, "We All Believe in One True God." This hymn is particularly important in Lutheran history because it's how Lutherans of old sang the faith to one another week after week.

> We all believe in one true God,
>   Who created earth and heaven,
> The Father, who to us in love
>   Has the right of children given.
> He in soul and body feeds us;
>   All we need His hand provides us;
> Through all snares and perils leads us,
>   Watching that no harm betide us,
> He cares for us by day and night;
> All things are governed by His might.
>
> We all believe in Jesus Christ,
>   His own Son, our Lord, possessing
> An equal Godhead, throne, and might,
>   Source of ev'ry grace and blessing;
> Born of Mary, virgin mother,
>   By the power of the Spirit,
> Word made flesh, our elder brother;
>   That the lost might life inherit,

---

6. *All God's People Sing!* (St. Louis: Concordia Publishing House, 1992) added six stanzas to the hymn that do indeed tell the full story of Jesus' incarnation, birth, Baptism, ministry, suffering and death, resurrection, and ascension.

Was crucified for all our sin
And raised by God to life again.

We all confess the Holy Ghost,
  Who, in highest heaven dwelling
With God the Father and the Son,
  Comforts us beyond all telling;
Who the Church, His own creation,
  Keeps in unity of spirit.
Here forgiveness and salvation
  Daily come through Jesus' merit.
All flesh shall rise, and we shall be
In bliss with God eternally.
  Amen.

—LSB 954

People have sometimes criticized Luther for putting the Creed into a prose paraphrase (though he based the tune and the text upon a pre-Reformation model); but Luther's great concern wasn't some kind of liturgical law. He wanted people to know, love, and confess the triune God. He had the wisdom to know that putting something to music and in rhymed verse enables people to learn it by heart, almost effortlessly with a bit of repetition. I would bet that most folks in those days knew the paraphrases they sung in church better than they knew even the explanations they memorized from the catechism.

The Creed as a witnessing tool shows up in the Large Catechism. Luther clearly saw the Creed as the solution to the question: "Who is your God?" He broke down the explanation to be so clear even a child could say it: He is my Father who made me; He is my Redeemer, my Lord, the Son who bought me; He is the Holy Spirit who makes me holy.

If, for example, one were to ask a young child, "My boy, what kind of God do you have? What do you know about Him?" then he could say, "First, my God is the Father who made heaven and earth. I take nothing and no one else as God except Him alone, for there simply is no one else who could have made heaven and earth." (Janzow 68)

The Creed as a means of witnessing our faith resonates deeply with me from my own journey into the Church. My parents had been Methodists, but they only attended church when they "went home" to their parents' farms in Virginia for the odd weekend. We lived an hour and a half away in Maryland. They never had me baptized as a child, though Mom did read me some Bible stories. Church, though, was not a regular part of life.

One day as a young teen, a friend invited me to attend his ballgame and watch him play. Sports have never been my thing, and I remember being rather bored as I watched. Two kids next to me struck up a conversation. They asked me if I knew what I needed to know in order to be saved. I remember being befuddled. They began reciting to me what I later realized was the Apostles' Creed. Those two young men were Roman Catholics. When I came home that day, I asked my mom what we were. I was told in no uncertain terms that we were not Catholic, but Protestant. That sent me to the *World Book Encyclopedia*, my constant companion in those days, and I read up a bit. I asked Mom about the Lutherans, since they were the first ones mentioned in the article on Protestants. As it turns out, our neighbors just two doors up attended the Lutheran Church in the neighborhood, and it was within walking distance. I showed up at that church one week, and I was baptized only a couple

> MY WHOLE JOURNEY INTO THE CHURCH STARTED WITH TWO YOUNG MEN SHARING THEIR FAITH USING THE APOSTLES' CREED.

of weeks after that. But my whole journey into the Church started with two young men sharing their faith using the Apostles' Creed.

So, whether it is Luther's paraphrase of the Nicene Creed that we still use in Divine Service, Setting Five or whether it is the simple Apostles' Creed, the Creeds are treasures that enable us to express our faith to others with confidence and simplicity. And this witness is authentic because it is animated by our joy in knowing the One whom we confess and introduce to others. Jesus is always at the heart of it.

We could point to any other number of hymns that we sing together that do a similar job. They give us words to express our delight and joy in the all-surpassing gift that we have encountered in the Lord. I especially think of the clear invitation expressed in the many hymns that call out, "Come!"

Think of it:

"O come, all ye faithful, joyful and triumphant!" (*LSB* 379).

"Come, your hearts and voices raising, Christ the Lord with gladness praising" (*LSB* 375).

"Come to Calv'ry's holy mountain, Sinners, ruined by the fall" (*LSB* 435).

"Come, you faithful, raise the strain Of triumphant gladness!" (*LSB* 487).

"The Bridegroom soon will call us, 'Come to the wedding feast'" (*LSB* 514).

"Come, let us join our cheerful songs With angels round the throne" (*LSB* 812).

With this "come," we urge each other on to enter into the praises of the Lord, that is, to enjoy Him—to taste and see that He is good.

And our witnessing out in the world can and should simply be an extension of that urging each other on to praise Him and taste His goodness, like in the hymns of the Church.

How beautifully this is described in the last chapter of Revelation:

> *The Spirit and the Bride say, "Come." And let the one who hears say, "Come." And let the one who is thirsty come; let the one who desires take the water of life without price.* *(Revelation 22:17)*

So the Christian witness is enjoying the Savior and His gifts, being awed by the way He so deeply exposes the wounds of our hearts and yet so gently pours His forgiveness, mercy, and healing on us. Then it cannot help but praise this Savior to others and invite them to meet Him: "Come and see!"

The key to becoming an authentic witness to Christ isn't found in practicing a technique; it cannot be found that way at all. Instead, it's found in tasting deeply of the goodness of the Lord for yourself—early and often—so that you will spontaneously cry out to others: "Oh, taste and see that the LORD is good!" For you know yourself how good He is.

FOR DISCUSSION

1. Explain in your own words the connection between enjoying something and praising it to others.

4. Why did Luther think the Creed provides a great witnessing tool?

2. How does Philip overcome Nathanael's initial skepticism?

5. When we invite others to "come" and take the water of life without price, what are we inviting them to?

3. How do the hymns we sing together often direct our witness?

CHAPTER 7

THE SEVENTH GODLY HABIT:
Watching for the Good Works God Has Prepared for Us to Do

If you think back to your childhood, perhaps you remember excitement on Easter morning. Not just a basket of goodies, ready prepared with chocolate bunnies, chocolate eggs, and marshmallow chicks. Those were great too, but what I am talking about is the hunt on Easter morning! The hunt for Easter eggs. Picture yourself for a moment again as a little one, with a basket in hand, toddling off. Can you hear yourself squeal in delight when you spy a colored egg peeking out from under a bush? You run to get it, put it in your basket, and then, eager-eyed, you search the horizon for another one. And another.

Have you ever thought of good works like that? They are wonderful little surprises that God has strewn all around us to delight us and give us Easter joy as we do them. Is not this how St. Paul describes good works in Ephesians 2?

> *And you were dead in the trespasses and sins in which you once walked . . . by nature children of wrath, like the rest of mankind. But God, being rich in mercy, because of the great love with which He loved us, even when we were dead in our trespasses, made us alive together with Christ—by grace you have been saved—and raised*

> us up with Him and seated us with Him in the heavenly
> places in Christ Jesus, so that in the coming ages He might
> show the immeasurable riches of His grace in kindness to-
> ward us in Christ Jesus. For by grace you have been saved
> through faith. And this is not your own doing; it is the gift
> of God, not a result of works, so that no one may boast. For
> we are His workmanship, created in Christ Jesus for good
> works, which God prepared beforehand, that we should
> walk in them. (Ephesians 2:1–2, 3–10, emphasis added)

Paul couldn't be any clearer: No, your good works don't save you.
Rather, God saves you, by grace, through faith—and even that faith
isn't something you come up with. No, it is His gift to you. God is
the doer of the verbs! He creates you anew through resurrection with
Christ to a new life (through Baptism), also creating you anew for good
works. He even prepares these good
works for you beforehand. Long before
you see the opportunity for good works
or recognize it, it was in God's heart as
a gift for you. By that good work, He
lets you exercise the resurrection life
planted into you at your Baptism. That
means that all around you every single
day, in your different callings, a huge variety of "Easter eggs" await your
discovery and enjoyment. Do you see how this sets everything on its
head? We like to think of good works as works that we do for God's
sake. That's backwards! Good works are actually gifts that God gives us.

> BY THAT GOOD WORK,
> HE LETS YOU EXERCISE
> THE RESURRECTION LIFE
> PLANTED INTO YOU AT
> YOUR BAPTISM.

What is the essence of these good works, these gracious opportunities to live the resurrection life? It boils down to one word, so abused
and misunderstood: love. By "love," I do not at all mean the emotional
high that people often think of: Hollywood's vacuous kind of love. It
is, rather, God's love for us in Christ Jesus that stirs us to love and care

for one another. This love helps us perceive that the opportunity to serve and do good is a gift handed to us from the Father who by this gift is inviting us to get in on the spreading of His own love.

To train ourselves to perceive and recognize the "Easter eggs" that our Heavenly Father has planted around us, we can turn to two related parts of the catechism: the Ten Commandments and the Table of Duties. Both open our eyes to see all the gifts that surround us every day, just waiting for us to discover and enjoy them.

Let's run through both of these parts of the catechism briefly with the help of Luther's explanations. First, the Ten Commandments. Here, you will note that good works really are of two kinds: those of the First Table (Commandments 1–3) and those of the Second Table (Commandments 4–10); that is, those focused on God and those focused on our neighbor.

FIRST TABLE OF THE LAW

The **First Commandment** itself is the undercurrent beneath each of the other Commandments to such an extent that the rest of the Commandments describe what life really looks like when a person has no other gods but the real One. Commandments 2 through 10 paint a picture in vivid detail of what it means to fear, love, and trust in God above all things. In doing so, they also provide a description of the life of our Lord Jesus. He alone kept all of the Commandments perfectly, and He kept them perfectly for us.

The **Second Commandment** (in Lutheran reckoning) is "You shall not misuse the name of the Lord your God." Luther unpacks this in the Small Catechism in both a positive and negative way, following the approach to the Law that Jesus reveals in His famous Sermon on the Mount (see Matthew 5–7). It seems odd, when you think about it, to say that *not* doing something could be a good work. We need to remember, though, that the "not doing" in every single instance in Luther's explanations is a refraining from, a refusing to abuse a gift.

The negative statements in Luther's explanations are about not seizing something and using it in a way that God Himself, the original Giver, never intended. Thus, each negative is a fence around something beautiful, something quite positive and joyful.

In the case of the Second Commandment, that beautiful thing is the name of the Lord your God. Remember that the word we usually render "Lord" is actually the four Hebrew letters, "YHWH," probably pronounced "Yahweh." This is God's specially revealed covenant name, disclosed to Moses at the burning bush (see Exodus 3). Yahweh is God's proper name, if you will. And we are using that name when we say in English, "Lord." He does not reveal His name to us for us to abuse or misuse it.

How might we misuse it? The catechism teaches us that because we fear and love God, we ought not "curse, swear, use satanic arts [literally, witchcraft], lie, or deceive by His name." Let's think about each of those: to curse is to use God's name to call down divine wrath on someone. If you've ever said, "Go to hell!" or "God damn you!" you have cursed. Swearing here is not referring to using unsavory four-letter words, but rather the frivolous use of God's name to back up the veracity of what we say. This doesn't mean that swearing is absolutely forbidden. Our Lord and St. Paul both allowed themselves to be placed under oath. But when you hear the casual, "I swear to God, if you buy me that, I'll be so happy!" that is an abuse of God's name. Jesus warns in the Sermon on the Mount (see Matthew 5:37) that the impulse to add the "I swear" comes from the evil one. Using God's name for witchcraft of any kind is a horrific abuse because it ignores the Person who gave us that name and tries to treat Him as a manipulable and impersonal force. This is what Simon the magician in Acts 8 attempted when he wanted to purchase the ability to give the Holy Spirit by the laying on of his hands. To lie or deceive by God's name can occur when we perjure ourselves in court. It also happens, though, when we say things about God that are not true (things that the Scriptures did not reveal) and insist that they are true. Luther rightly regards this as the worst abuse of God's name.

So that is the negative part of the explanation, the "fence" around the Second Commandment. What about the gift itself, the proper use of God's name? Luther says we are to "call upon it in every trouble, pray, praise, and give thanks." That is, God's name is given to you so that you know to whom to turn when you are facing a trouble or hardship, when you or others need anything, or when you experience a special joy and want to thank the Giver of that gift.

Think for a moment about the wedding at Cana. Mary, the mother of Jesus, became aware of her neighbor's need. The wine had run out! It was about to be a shame and disgrace for the family of the bride. So look at what Mary does. She takes her neighbor's need into her heart, carries it to her Son, and then dumps it squarely at His feet. Here is a trouble that she cannot fix; but what is there that her

> HERE IS A TROUBLE THAT SHE CANNOT FIX; BUT WHAT IS THERE THAT HER SON CANNOT FIX?

Son cannot fix? She doesn't tell Him how she thinks He should fix it, or when. She just prays (if you will), and leaves it entirely in His hand. That is what it is to call upon God in trouble! God invites us, "Call upon Me in the day of trouble; I will deliver you, and you shall glorify Me" (Psalm 50:15).

And what does it look like to give thanks? We know the goodness of the beauty of a rose, a stunning sunset, the refreshing sip of cold water from a spring, the bracing taste of your coffee enjoyed in the morning, the look on the face of your child as she sleeps. For all of these: "Praise You, Lord!" The good work is to acknowledge and name the Giver of the gift, the Deliverer from every trouble we will ever face. This is the proper use of God's name, and the opportunities to use it in this way surround us on every hand. "Easter eggs" galore!

The ***Third Commandment*** was described extensively in the first chapter, so we won't repeat what was said there. We will note, though, that attending to the Word (chapter 1) is precisely what enables the keeping of Commandments 1 and 2; for in the Word, faith (i.e., fear, love, and trust in God) is given, and the Giver of all good introduces Himself to us and teaches us how to rightly use His name.

SECOND TABLE OF THE LAW

With the Second Table of the Law, we begin to recognize the gifts of God that come through others and how we may serve God by serving others. It starts with the people closest to us, those through whom God gave us our very existence, our life itself: our parents. The ***Fourth Commandment***: "Honor your father and your mother."

Luther argues in the Large Catechism that God places parents in a particularly exalted position by commanding more than love. He commands honor. "For to honor is a much higher thing than to love, for honor includes not only love but also respect, humility, and awe, directed, one might say, toward a hidden majesty of theirs" (Janzow 29). What does this honor include? Here is how Luther explains it:

> **It means that you are above all to prize and value them as earth's greatest treasure. Next, in speaking to them you are to behave respectfully, never address them in a rude, taunting, or challenging matter [*sic*], but give in to them and hold your tongue even when they go too far. Third, by means of your actions, both physical and financial, you are to show them honor by serving them, helping them, and providing for them when they are old, sick, infirm, or poor. All this you should do not only willingly but also with humility and respect as one who is under the scrutiny of God. (Janzow 30)**

Additionally, Luther sees in the vocation of parents the grounding of all authority in our communal life, thus recognizing that the family is the basic building block of the entire society. From this, he argues that teachers at school stand *in loco parentis* ("in place of the parents"), as do employers, government officials, and even church authorities. All of these vocations reflect an aspect of fatherhood and, therefore, deserve to be honored. In sum, "earthly authority . . . all comes under the heading of the parental office and radiates outward from it in all directions" (Janzow 36). Luther places this work of honoring parents and authorities in the highest position of good works: "Not even gifts of charity nor any other service rendered to the neighbor can equal this work. For God has given the highest ranking to parenthood, making it, in fact, His representative on earth" (Janzow 33). Yes, charity really does start at home! If your parents are still alive, your relationship with them is a great place to discover the "Easter egg" of good works. What can you do to surprise and bless your parents and show them how grateful you are that through them God gave your very life? That through them He clothed you, fed you, and nourished you when you would have perished in your hunger and your own filth without them? If you are a parent, this commandment reminds you of the high honor of being God's fellow worker when you procreate, and then the high honor you carry as the one responsible to tend and nourish your children and bring them up in the faith as God's own representative in their lives. Changing diapers, feeding hungry mouths, clothing naked bodies, teaching little ones how to receive all things as gifts from the Father who loves them through Jesus. These are good works of the highest order, according to the Fourth Commandment. In the home, good works simply overflow and abound.

One final word about the good works described by the Fourth Commandment: there are times when parents utterly fail in their duty toward their children; times even when they betray their children and abuse them. If you have been through that pain, you know how devastating it is; it gives an incredibly deep wound to the human heart. The Fourth Commandment reveals to you that what you experienced is not what God intended for our lives. Yet, even through your parent was so sinful and damaging to you, he or she has still given you the good gift of life, and none of his or her sins against you can take that truth away. You, then, are called by the Fourth Commandment to honor your parents for the office, the work of giving you life, that God did through them, not their abuse of that office. The same is true concerning those who abuse their God-given authority in any office: a boss, a teacher, a government leader. That person's abuse of the office does not give us the freedom to despise the office; it gives us the opportunity to recognize that a good gift of God intended for our blessing has been corrupted. We still honor the office as the good gift; but we may certainly deplore the wrongs done in its abuse.

Concerning the **Fifth Commandment**, "You shall not murder," Luther observes: "In this next commandment we shall step outside of our own home and go out among our neighbors to learn how we and they should live together, how each one individually should conduct himself toward his fellow man" (Janzow 41). The Small Catechism summarizes the entirety of this commandment with, "We should fear and love God so that we do not hurt or harm our neighbor in his body, but help and support him in every physical need."

Jesus' famous parable of the Good Samaritan helps us think about the importance of the breadth of the Fifth Commandment in our lives. A man going down from Jerusalem to Jericho was beaten up by bandits and left naked and half dead. That man was an "Easter egg," an opportunity for a gift, waiting to be discovered. But the blindness of the priest and of the Levite prevented them from seeing the gift at all. All they saw was a nuisance and possibly a danger for themselves—for the old Adam is always paralyzed by fear. What they missed was that the very suffering of the man in front of them was a gift to them, a way that God desired to call them out of their innate constant self-preoccupation, to call them to the side of another human being with compassion. Compassion is that gut-wrenching ache when you so acutely share in another's suffering that you taste it as your own and hasten to do everything you can to ease their pain. Opportunities to have compassion are a gift because doing good works is an essential part of a healthy, living Christian faith. This will sound heretical but it isn't: good works will never save you, but good works are the embodiment of salvation as it leads you down love's path (see Philippians 2:12–13).

When the Samaritan saw the man, he had compassion, Jesus said. The Samaritan went to the man. That is, he didn't pass by the "Easter egg," preoccupied with his own thoughts and plans or fears and insecurities. Rather, his compassion brought him to the side of the injured man. Yes, he poured oil and wine on the man's wounds, put the injured man on his own beast, and provided for the man's further care in an inn. The great miracle, though, was right there at the start. The Samaritan had compassion. He went to the helpless stranger. He took the sorrows of the victim right into his own heart. He did this though he wasn't of the same people or nation, while the priest and Levite in the story were of the same nationality and ethnic group as the victim.

Jesus tells this story in Luke 10 to a man who wishes "to justify himself" by narrowing down the scope of the word "neighbor." "Who is my neighbor?" he asks Jesus. Jesus' story invites a whole different question. It invites the question, "Am I a neighbor? When I see the bodily need of other human beings, do I see that they are my own brothers and sisters? Can I realize that in their need, God is giving me the gift of seeing them for who they truly are—creatures made in God's image, redeemed by Jesus Christ, just like me?" Jesus' story makes us reflect on whether we act in accord with what Paul says to the Athenians, "[God] made from one man every nation of mankind to live on all the face of the earth. . . . He is actually not far from each one of us" (Acts 17:26–27).

The Fathers of the Church often declared that the wounded man in the parable of the Good Samaritan was Adam (and therefore also all of us who have descended from Adam), and the Second Adam, Jesus, was the one whose compassion came to the side of the wounded man to provide for his healing. Therefore, in that reading of the story, Jesus, our Good Samaritan, tells the story to begin to open our eyes. The sorrows, the sufferings, the heartaches of the sons of Adam and the daughters of Eve enlivened Jesus' compassion; and we, following our Lord and Savior, also allow the sorrows and sufferings of others to stir our compassion. Others' sufferings call out to us. And we find that when we answer that call, when we have compassion and go to others in their time of need, not only do we help them, but we ourselves are also richly blessed. Every. Single. Time.

I have an amazing father-in-law. He, Dave, has Good Samaritan eyes. The other night we were talking at dinner. He is contemplating getting his left shoulder operated on. Three years ago, he had his right shoulder done. For rehab, he went to our local Lutheran retirement/rehabilitation/nursing home. There, he met a woman from a nearby town who had a rough go after a surgery. He casually mentioned that sometimes he stops in to see how she's doing now that she's home, and he's happy to report that she is doing well. To my shame, I confess, as Dave was telling this story, my first thought was, "Why on earth do you bother keeping up with someone you met by chance briefly at a rehab center?" Then the full weight of my impoverished thinking dawned on me.

How much I miss in life because I do not look with Good Samaritan eyes! How many wonderful people God has tried to give me as sisters and brothers and companions in life's journey, and I have been blind to them and blind to their needs? Like the priest and the Levite in Jesus' story, I have often stepped

> How much I miss in life because I do not look with Good Samaritan eyes!

around (sometimes quite literally!) the "Easter eggs" that God plants all around me for me to discover, rejoice in, and thank Him for.

Of course, it is not just dire need and intense suffering that creates "Easter eggs." Sometimes it is a simple need, something that just needs a helping hand. My pastor likes to tell a story of seeing a young father juggling his child in his arms while trying to get coffee from the church coffee urn; all the while, he was talking to another man with empty hands. The other fellow never even noticed the young father's dilemma! Surely taking the cup and filling it and giving it back with a smile would have been an act of kindness to the harried dad. But even more, it would be a blessing to the other man as he realized, "God put me right here at this very moment to be able to be a blessing to my brother! What a great God He is that He cares about even these moments in our lives!"

In the **Sixth Commandment**, we see that even more "Easter eggs" are waiting for us. Because God made marriage between a man and a woman the foundation on which He would build society, He gives a particular commandment that guards and protects their union and oneness. "You shall not commit adultery." What does this mean? "We should fear and love God so that we lead a sexually pure and decent life in what we say and do, and husband and wife love and honor each other." "Sexually pure" used to be rendered "chaste" in the Small Catechism. I like that much better. Chastity is actually bigger than "sexual purity." At its root, it recognizes the dignity and honor of the human body, formed by God and intended to be the temple of the Holy Spirit. This is true for my own body and as well as for the bodies of everyone else. Chastity means recognizing that the body was made for the Lord. This commandment invites us, above all, to stop seeing other people as mere objects for our use and abuse; it unfolds for us that they are persons! If you think about lust, it most certainly is not interested in the other as a person at all. It wants to use their body and then be free to discard them. Think of the terrible story in Scripture of

Amnon's rape of Tamar (see 2 Samuel 13). He was obsessed with her body and wanted her, but as soon as he had her, he threw her away, dismissed her without any interest in her well-being. What he wanted was his own gratification without any regard for the person before him. He seemed oblivious not only to what would hurt and harm her, but also to how treating another human being in this fashion degraded and abused his own body.

In our day, online pornography is a massive epidemic. It reaches its tentacles out to ensnare every one of us. What is wrong with it? Have you ever thought about that? What is so damaging about porn? It is so damaging precisely because those who use it are not the least bit interested in the people they see acting on the screen. There is no concern for the persons they see; no concern about their best interest. The people portrayed in porn are objects for one's own pleasure; they are used, seen in a way completely divorced from relationship, and then are clicked away when one is through with them. Just like Amnon using Tamar and then dismissing her. The effect of this is that you become locked up inside yourself. The gift of sexuality, this great gift, was meant to lead you out of yourself to realize that another person stands before you to be loved and celebrated, valued and received as a gift from the hand of the Father. Saying no to online porn is part of saying a firm yes to the real people in our lives and treating them as persons, not as objects for your possession and use. Every last person you encounter meets you as a gift to be received. Each is called to be a son or daughter of God, a temple of His Spirit. If you can help people see by the way you treat them the dignity they have because of who they are in relationship to God, you soon realize that this is also a blessing to you, an "Easter egg" waiting to be enjoyed.

All of this applies whether you are married or single—even living a single life consecrated to God and not looking for marriage. Is fire good, or is fire bad? Obviously, it depends. If the fire is in the fireplace, warming the home on a cold winter's night, it is good and very good.

If the fire is outside the fireplace, burning the house down, it is bad and very bad. The fireplace in the analogy is the marriage bed, and the fire is the gift of the one-flesh union between a man and a woman that comes through sex. For married persons to honor the personhood of their spouse by that union which is holy in God's eyes is to do a good work (see 1 Corinthians 7:1–5). For the single person to refrain from using his or her body in a way that treats others merely as objects is to do a good work. The honoring of the bodies and therefore the personhood of others while also honoring one's own self by who one is united with is at the heart of the Sixth Commandment.

While God uses the Fifth and Sixth Commandments to teach us to no longer think of people as "things," we learn in the **Seventh Commandment** that bona fide "things" in life usually are attached to people. The Small Catechism teaches us that the commandment "you shall not steal" involves a lot more than just a "sneak thief" taking something that belongs to another person. "We should fear and love God so that we do not take our neighbor's money or possessions, or get them in any dishonest way, but help him to improve and protect his possessions and income." In the Large Catechism, Luther teaches that God desires us not to cheat our neighbor out of his money or stuff, even when doing so could be "legal." Price gouging in the marketplace, shoddy workmanship, and shady business deals are all ways that people violate the Seventh Commandment. What is the "Easter egg"? What is the good, the hidden blessing that the commandment enjoins? Opportunities to help our neighbor actually improve and protect his possessions and income.

Another story about my father-in-law: It was a cold and blustery winter day. The snow had been falling all day and was still falling. You could hear the wind beating up against the house. We had just finished dinner. The kids were in bed and the adults were ready to sit down to play some cards. Then the phone rang. My father-in-law answered it. It was an elderly lady to whom he and my mother-in-law used to live next door. The woman's children were spending the holidays abroad, and she was worried. She kept hearing a strange sound on the side of the house during this storm. My father-in-law told her, "We'll drive over and check it out." He gathered some tools and his sons-in-laws and out we headed into the storm. When we got there, we trudged in the snow around to the side of the house and immediately saw the problem. The wind, whipping as it was, had loosened some of the vinyl siding, and the siding was now flapping in the wind. That's what the woman had been hearing.

Not having very good "Easter egg" eyes, I assumed we would just tell her, "It's nothing too serious; your kids will just need to call someone to fix it. There are three pieces loose on the second story." Wrong, wrong, wrong. My father-in-law doesn't miss an "Easter egg." "Boys," he said, "let's get the ladder from around back."

Now, you have to understand that two of us are completely useless when it comes to practical, handyman things like this. As the three of us set up the ladder, two of us told the third, my electrician brother-in-law, that we'd be happy to hold the ladder while he went up. The repair only took a short time. The vinyl was secured so that it was no longer flapping and so that no further damage would be done. The elderly woman was quite grateful. I received another lesson in the true greatness of my father-in-law, who simply has "Easter egg" eyes and happily goes forth to discover the "Easter eggs" in front of him. His neighbor needed help with her possessions, and he simply went right there to help, eager and happy to be of service. As we drove home, I remember I had the odd feeling that the elderly woman had done me a favor that night.

But of course, our neighbor needs help not just with his stuff, but also with his reputation, with preserving his good name. Hence the **_Eighth Commandment_**: "You shall not give false testimony against your neighbor." What does this mean? "We should fear and love God so that we do not tell lies about our neighbor, betray him, slander him, or hurt his reputation, but defend him, speak well of him, and explain everything in the kindest way" (Small Catechism, Eighth Commandment). This commandment warns us first of all against lying. The psalmist confesses, "All mankind are liars" (Psalm 116:11). To those who did not accept Jesus' words, Jesus said that they were of their father, the devil, who "has nothing to do with the truth, because there is no truth in him. When he lies, he speaks out of his own character, for he is a liar and the father of lies" (John 8:44). The old self in the Christian is by nature a liar. He likes to make himself appear in a better light than what is reality. And he very much enjoys when others appear in a worse light than he does. "Human nature is infected with this common disease, that one rather hears evil than good about one's neighbor. And though we ourselves are evil, we cannot stand to have anyone speak evil of us. Every one of us would like all the world to say nothing about him but words of golden goodwill; yet we cannot bear it when we hear the best spoken of others" (Janzow 54).

Ouch. That is so true. But God's "Easter egg" in the Eighth Commandment encompasses more than just refraining from lying with our tongues. Our Father also wants to protect our neighbor from the harm we would do to him by sharing his secrets (betraying him), slandering him, or hurting his reputation in any way. This "Easter egg" also involves being proactive to build a good reputation for our neighbor: to use our tongue to "defend him, speak well of him, and explain everything in the kindest way."

Imagine you are at work one day, and the boss is out of earshot. Your co-workers start to gripe about her. What do you do? Here's your "egg"! It is a chance for you to speak up for your boss and, above all, to explain your boss's actions in a kind way that your co-workers may not have thought of before.

The name *Satan* means "the accuser." When we join Satan in accusing each other, we are missing the gift God is putting before us in that moment: the joy of defending our neighbor over against

Satan's accusations. Remember that the Second and Third Persons of the Trinity both share the title "Paraclete" or "Advocate." Rather than accuse us before the Father, the members of the Trinity defend us! And this particular joy is what the Eighth Commandment offers to us: the opportunity to share in this job of the Son and Spirit because we are a new creation, resurrected to life in Christ.

The **Ninth Commandment** warns us against coveting our neighbor's house, the **Tenth** against coveting our neighbor's wife, workers, or animals. The catechism again explains these both in terms of negative and positive actions. Negatively, we are not to "scheme to get our neighbor's inheritance or house, or get it in a way which only appears right." Similarly, we are not to "entice or force away our neighbor's wife, workers, or animals, or turn them against him" in disloyalty. Positively, we are to "help and be of service" to our neighbor in keeping his inheritance and house. We are also to urge our neighbor's wife, his workers, and animals "to stay and do their duty" (Small Catechism, Ninth Commandment, Tenth Commandment).

Our Lord confronts the danger of coveting head-on when He says, "Take care, and be on your guard against all covetousness, for one's life does not consist in the abundance of his possessions" (Luke 12:15). The temptation always is to think that one's life, one's very joy and livelihood, hangs on either stuff or relationships with other people. "I could be happy if only I had . . ." How many times do we have to fall into this trap before we will see it for what it is?

I have a knife I like to keep close at hand, a hunting knife. It's rather rusted, but it serves me well every time I look at it. You see, I was a youngest child. I knew exactly how to work my parents to get what I wanted. Once, when I was a youngster, we visited my cousins down in the country in Virginia (we lived in the DC suburbs in Maryland). My cousins had just gotten new hunting knives. I was immediately transfixed by these knives. I just had to have one. I had the hour and a half riding home in the car to work on my dad. I don't think we had reached the halfway mark before he turned around and shouted, "If you will just stop nagging me about it, I'll get you a knife." I think I had the chutzpah to say, "Today? Can we go today?" Yes, I was that bad. And I remember selecting it and carrying it out of the store, trying to disguise the disappointment. "Oh. So this is what I really wanted. A knife. How nice. Now I have it."

Would you care to guess how many times I've actually ever used that knife? You'd be right if you said zero. I did leave it out in the rain once; therefore the rust. But I keep it close at hand because it reminds me: "Weedon, happiness doesn't come from getting things." Remember that. I try to think of my knife whenever the latest Apple gadget comes out and entices me.

What is the good that Commandments 9 and 10 seek to guard? Contentment! St. Paul could boast to the Philippians that he had learned the secret of contentment. He knew how to abound and how to be abased. He could do all things through Christ who gave him strength. He had discovered that if he had Jesus, he truly had everything anyone could ever need. Being content, then, he was free to receive and rejoice in whatever gifts others gave him. He was also so free that he didn't fret when he had very little. He knew whatever he had was always enough with the Lord. The Ninth and Tenth Commandments open our eyes to the "Easter eggs" disguised as life's little blessings that we all too often take for granted and overlook: a home that shelters us, a family who loves us, friends who sweeten our lives, and food and drink that we enjoy together.

TABLE OF DUTIES

The third section of the Small Catechism explores various arenas in which the good works that God sets before us occur. Concerning duties in the Church, there are two categories in this section: Bishops, Pastors, and Preachers and then Hearers. In the civil realm, there are instructions for both those who govern and those who are citizens. In the house, there are special duties for husbands, for wives, for parents, and for children. For the workplace, there are instructions for both those who supervise others and those who are supervised—and very often we are both. Then words are included for the young and for widows, and then finally, there is a word for everyone, no matter his or her station in life. The catechism significantly teaches that all of these are "various holy orders and positions," and it lists out the Scriptures appropriate for each of the various callings' "duties and responsibilities."

That all these orders in life are truly holy orders is one of the profound insights of Reformation theology. While Christians in the Middle Ages certainly would have understood the bishop in his office of preaching and teaching to be in a holy order, it was a brand new thought that the average Christian hearer also occupied a holy order and was engaged in a good work by listening to the Word and by supporting the ministry of preaching and teaching with their gifts. Similarly, it was quite the surprise to them that civil government in punishing evil and protecting those who do right is a holy order and doing a good work. And that being a citizen is a holy order; when he or she cheerfully pays taxes to and prays for the government officials, it is a good work, well pleasing to God. Husbands and wives together actually live in a most holy order: marriage. When they sacrifice together for the good of their family, they perform a good work. To be a child is in itself a holy order and when a child cheerfully sweeps the floor at the parent's bidding, a veritable and precious good work has been done. Workers stand in a holy order and offer the sacrifice of serving their employers, not by mere appearance, but with singleness of heart, doing their work as if doing it for Christ. Being young is a holy order in which one is called upon to do the good work of respecting the aged. Widows in their holy order devote themselves to prayer. And everyone in every order is to always seek to love and live in constant prayer. The Table of Duties provides a great place to look for the particular "Easter eggs" God has strewn in the path of your vocations.

Such "Easter eggs" are too many to enumerate; but once we have the eyes to see them, we are simply shocked at the lavishness of God's planning in putting them all around us from the start to the end of the day. Yes, it reaches all the way to the mom or dad, who wrinkles the nose and realizes that God is giving them the gift of changing that dirty diaper to serve this little person who is so helpless, so dependent on them. And it reaches to getting ready to put a cup in the dishwasher only to discover it is all clean, and therefore emptying everything, putting all of the dishes away, unasked. It includes noticing that a neighbor has been having a rough go and cutting his or her grass to help eliminate one task off of his or her hectic list. Or it involves sitting down with a colleague who seems upset and asking them if they want to talk.

> SUCH "EASTER EGGS" ARE TOO MANY TO ENUMERATE; BUT ONCE WE HAVE THE EYES TO SEE THEM, WE ARE SIMPLY SHOCKED AT THE LAVISHNESS OF GOD'S PLANNING IN PUTTING THEM ALL AROUND US FROM THE START TO THE END OF THE DAY.

What is the most wonderful thing about learning to live this "Easter egg" hunt sort of life? This sort of life ends up leading others to praise the heavenly Father. This is exactly what Jesus was getting at when He told the disciples in the Sermon on the Mount: "You are the light of the world. A city set on a hill cannot be hidden. Nor do people light a lamp and put it under a basket, but on a stand, and it gives light to all in the house. In the same way, let your light shine before others, so that they may see your good works and give glory to your Father who is in heaven" (Matthew 5:14–16). "Easter eggs" are the opposite of practicing your righteousness before other people in order to be seen and noticed by them. They are not focused on how pious you are; they are simply all about love. Being "other" focused. Seeing a need and seeing the person behind the need; and honoring them by helping in whatever ways you can, big or small. "Easter eggs" abounding!

FOR DISCUSSION

1. Why does God want the Christian to do good works?

2. Why is "Easter egg" an apt description of the good works God has prepared for us to do?

We get joy
god gives us these gifts

3. In what ways are the Ten Commandments useful for recognizing the surprising good works that God plants all around for us to do?

both open our eyes to see the gifts all around us.

4. What are some of the good works that you see God has planted for you in the First Table of the Law?

fear, love, trust in god.

5. What are some of the good works that you see God has planted for you in the Second Table of the Law?

Serve God by serving others!

6. How does the Table of Duties expand the concept of "holy orders and positions"?

7. What particular "holy orders and positions" have you been called to in your life?

8. How do good works cultivate doxology and praise to God?

CHAPTER 8

THE EIGHTH GODLY HABIT:
Remembering Death and the Day of Judgment

⟫●⟪

An ancient group of philosophers called the Stoics believed it was important for everyone to remember death each day. Their reasoning was, "You're going to die. You don't know when, but you know it will happen." Making people depressed was not the purpose of this, but rather helping people actually savor life and not sleepwalk through it. They also believed that if you remembered life's impermanence, you also would not be so quick to take your loved ones and friends for granted. Who knows, after all, how long you will have their company, and they yours? There is a good dose of common sense in this perspective.

Yet stoicism doesn't come anywhere close to plumbing the reasons why Christians, from early times, have also frequently and intentionally remembered death. Stoicism lacked a framework to truly see death as it is. To the Stoic, death was just a natural part of life: you are born, you grow old, and then you die. It seems to happen to everything that "lives" in this world. Death is just the concluding chapter of life.

Christians, however, remember the beginning: Genesis. We remember that death is not a "natural" part of the world because it is not what God intended for His creation. We remember that the Creator's gift was life, a life in which all things were good and very good. "Death" was at first only a word in God's new creation, part of a warning attached to the fruit of a tree. It had no concrete place in human existence until man wanted his way instead of God's and let the monster in and turned it loose. When Christians remember death, even remembering it daily, we're not merely recalling that there is a terminus to life that comes at an unexpected time. We're recalling that our first parents' disobedience let loose an enemy into the very fabric of creation and that it is even now at work in our own bodies and souls.

> WHEN CHRISTIANS REMEMBER DEATH, WE'RE RECALLING THAT OUR FIRST PARENTS' DISOBEDIENCE LET LOOSE AN ENEMY INTO THE VERY FABRIC OF CREATION AND THAT IT IS EVEN NOW AT WORK IN OUR OWN BODIES AND SOULS.

Have you ever wondered who told the truth that day in the garden? God had said, "The day that you eat of [the tree of the knowledge of good and evil] you shall surely die" (Genesis 2:17). The serpent contradicted that and said, "You will not surely die" (Genesis 3:4). So who was right? I loved to ask that of my Confirmation students in the past. They thoughtlessly answer, "God!" But then I would say, "Oh, really. Did Adam and Eve drop dead then and there?" Puckered brows. "The serpent?" they venture. The question provided a great intro to a discussion about how, for the Christian, death is not merely what happens when you stop breathing. Adam and Eve did not stop breathing the day they took the fruit, the one thing in all the creation that God had not given to them. If death is not just not breathing, what exactly was it that God meant with His warning in the garden? "The day that you eat of it you shall surely die." What, then, is it to die? What exactly is death?

One way to gain insight on this is to think of our Lord's parable of the prodigal son(s). Here, we learn what death is from *God's* perspective. You remember the story, I'm sure. The younger of two sons asked for the share of goods coming to him, went to "a far country," and wasted his inheritance in riotous living. Then, he came upon hard times and finally remembered and wanted to go home. He decided it was worth a try to come home and ask his father for mercy and to be treated like one of the hired hands of the family. He figured he had forfeited forever his right to be regarded as a son. But he understood so very little of his father's heart! He came home to the most shockingly grand and unexpected welcome and restoration into his father's house. The oldest brother was not amused, however, when he got wind of the reason for all of the hoopla. He stood outside, essentially pouting. The father found him and spoke incredibly tender words to him.

What interests us particularly are the final words of this parable. The father said to the elder son, "It was fitting to celebrate and be glad, for this your brother was dead, and is alive; he was lost, and is found" (Luke 15:32). What is death? The Father reveals it right here: death is wandering away from your Father. Death is losing the home that He prepared for you. Death is exiling yourself from His embrace and love.

> DEATH IS WANDERING AWAY FROM YOUR FATHER. DEATH IS LOSING THE HOME THAT HE PREPARED FOR YOU. DEATH IS EXILING YOURSELF FROM HIS EMBRACE AND LOVE.

Death is not nonexistence, but rather existence in "a far country"—that is, a long way from home.

Go back to Genesis 2 and 3 now and see it with a new light: "For in the day that you eat of it, you shall surely die" (Genesis 2:17). "You are dust and to dust you shall return" (Genesis 3:19). "Therefore the LORD God sent him out from the garden of Eden to work the ground from which he was taken. He drove out the man, and at the east of the garden of Eden he placed the cherubim and a flaming sword that turned every way to guard the way to the tree of life" (Genesis 3:23–24). Our first parents died the day they lost their home—the home God had made for them. They show that they had lost it even before he drives them out by their running and hiding and by no longer feeling comfortable in their nakedness (after all, home is where you *can* walk around in your birthday suit!). Their bodies are no longer the home in which they can experience God's gifts and become His temples. The sorrow of death, then, is essentially a sorrow of exile and homesickness. You can hear the lament of death itself in the song of the exiles from Psalm 137:

> *By the waters of Babylon, there we sat down and wept,*
> *when we remembered Zion. (Psalm 137:1)*

This is not *just* the song of the exiled Israelites. It expresses a truth that discloses the sorrow of the fallen human heart. We have lost our true home. And the story of our journey toward the grave is a story of progressive losses, mounting up, until at the end we lose even the body which cries to us at every turn that we once *had* a home that we no longer can find.

The Christian remembers all of this when he or she thinks of death. What we normally refer to as death—the cessation of breathing—is but a consequence and culmination of the exile into which every last one of us has been born.

So the exile is the bigger death of which the cessation of breathing and subsequent corruption is but the most visible manifestation. Adam and Eve entered that bigger death on the day they took the forbidden fruit; or more truthfully, that bigger death entered them.

Every Ash Wednesday, in countless congregations around the world, Christians line up and come forward to receive a strange mark, ashes smeared on their forehead, while hearing the words God spoke to Adam and Eve on the day death entered the human body. "Remember, O man, that you are dust and to dust you shall return." Remember. Remember each day how this journey to the grave all began, with the loss of our true home, exiled from our Father.

Yet on Ash Wednesday, the ashes are not placed in a single blob, but in the shape of a cross. This remembrance, then, is not only about being "dead men walking," headed to the grave. Rather it is also a remembrance that out of unfathomable love, there came forth from the Father His Only Son, into our flesh to know this exile, this death, in His own body, nailed to the cross—thereby opening for us once again the way home.

It was on the very night that His sufferings began that Jesus spoke to His disciples some astounding words:

> *Let not your hearts be troubled. Believe in God; believe also in Me. In My Father's house are many rooms. If it were not so, would I have told you that I go to prepare a place for you? And if I go and prepare a place for you, I will come again and will take you to Myself, that where I am you may be also. And you know the way to where I am going. (John 14:1–4)*

That is, Jesus said you have a home again. He said, "I am opening the way for you to come home. I am preparing to destroy your death by giving you 'a place.'" It sounded so good to the disciples; but Thomas was confused. He didn't understand where Jesus was going. He said, "Lord, we do not know where you are going. How can we know the way?" (John 14:5). Jesus' answer is one of His most famous sayings: "I am the way, and the truth, and the life. No one comes to the Father except through Me" (John 14:6).

Jesus not only provides the way to the home He has prepared; He also is the way. But how is He the way and how does He "prepare a place" for us? This is the marvel before which we will bow in adoration to all eternity. Theologians calls it "the blessed exchange." He prepared a way for us to come home and stay there forever by fully entering into the exile and loneliness away from Him that we chose. (This is why Jesus cried out on the cross, "Eli, Eli, lema sabachthani?" [Matthew 27:46].) He will go into the darkness and fill it with His very own light. He will

> **He will enter into our death to pour into it His own divine life, destroying death from the inside out.**

enter into our death to pour into it His own divine life, destroying death from the inside out.

When the Christian thinks of death daily, he or she also remembers this above all: that Jesus entered into death for us to knock a hole through death's stinking gullet and to open the way back to the home God created for us at the beginning. Thus, we sing:

My Savior, be Thou near me
When death is at my door;
Then let Thy presence cheer me,
Forsake me nevermore!
When soul and body languish,
O leave me not alone,
But take away mine anguish
By virtue of Thine own!

Be Thou my consolation,
My shield, when I must die;
Remind me of Thy passion
When my last hour draws nigh.
Mine eyes shall then behold Thee,
Upon Thy cross shall dwell,
My heart by faith enfold Thee.
Who dieth thus dies well.

—*LSB* 450:6–7

Because this is so, the Christian daily thinks of death in order to learn to think of it as a defeated foe. If through Christ, the way home has already been opened ("When You had overcome the sharpness of death, You opened the kingdom of heaven to all believers" [Te Deum]), then death itself has been truly robbed of its sting. The cessation of breathing that awaits all of us except the final generation who will be alive at Christ's glorious return has been thus transformed. What has the physical cessation of breathing we call "death" been transformed into?

We get a huge hint of how to reframe our thinking about this wretched enemy in Jesus' encounters with other people's deaths in the Gospels. In John 11, we learn that Jesus hears His dear friend Lazarus is sick and sick unto death. Lazarus's sisters, Mary and Martha, send word to Jesus, begging Him to come before it is too late. Jesus does the oddest thing, though. He tarries. He waits for four whole days. Then He tells His disciples, "Our friend Lazarus has fallen asleep, but I go to awaken him" (John 11:11). The disciples completely misunderstand and assume Jesus thinks Lazarus is just resting now and on the road to recovery. So Jesus makes the point more clear: "Lazarus has died, and for your sake I am glad that I was not there, so that you may believe. But let us go to him" (John 11:14–15).

In this story, Jesus teaches us that to Him, death is rather like a sound sleep, a rest from which His voice has the power to awaken us. He demonstrates this when He cries out loudly to Lazarus: "'Lazarus, come out.'" And "the man who had died came out" (John 11:43–44). And this is not the only instance when Jesus refers to death as sleep. We see this also when Jesus enters Jairus's house; the mourners are doing their ritual wailing, and the mother and father are heartbroken. What does Jesus tell them? "Why are you making a commotion and weeping? *The child is not dead but sleeping*" (Mark 5:39, emphasis added). So He calls her from death, takes her by the hand, and raises her.

This description of death as sleep then becomes a part of the way Christians speak, as a way of remembering that the resurrection of Christ has fundamentally changed how we must view this "last enemy." In 1 Corinthians 15, when Paul announces, "We shall not all sleep, but we shall all be changed" (1 Corinthians 15:51), he is proclaiming that not everyone will die; the generation that is alive when Christ returns will not die, but will be changed from mortal to immortal while still alive. Similarly, in 1 Thessalonians 4:15, Paul writes, "For this we declare to you by a word from the Lord, that we who are alive, who are left until the coming of the Lord, will not precede those who have fallen asleep," that is, those who have died. We will not all die. And even those who do, in fact only sleep; they will be raised again to new life. Their death is only temporary rest.

How beautifully Luther preached this when he dealt with the death of the son of the widow at Nain, the traditional Gospel reading for the Sixteenth Sunday after Trinity:

> The moment he speaks that one word, "Young man, I say unto thee, Arise!"; "Lazarus, come forth!"; "Talitha cumi, Damsel, I say unto thee, Arise!" they hear in that very instant. And on Judgment Day, when he speaks that one word, the dead will hear in that very same moment and come forth from the graves. It is true, *we sleep much more soundly in bed than we do in the churchyard!*

> Thus before our Lord God, death is not death but a sleep. For us, when we die it is and is termed death, but *before God it is but a sleep and a very light sleep at that.*

> Of this our dear Lord wants to convince us, so that we do not become frightened if pestilence, or death itself, approach, but learn to say, Death, what is the worst you can do to us? You have frightening teeth, you bare them and you terrify me, and I do not die gladly. But I don't want to consider only what you can do, and how, as you, like the executioner, draw the sword; but I want to ponder and perceive how our Lord God will intervene, even though you strangle me. He does not fear you, nor is he awed by

your raging and ravaging, but says, "Death, I shall be the death of you; grave, I shall be your destruction." (*Sermons of Martin Luther: The House Postils,* vol. III, ed. Eugene F. A. Klug, trans. Eugene F. A. Klug et al. [Grand Rapids: Baker Books, 1996], 32, emphasis added)

Yes, though to us death looks so final, it is not so at all to Jesus. His voice reaches the dead and wakes them more quickly than a mom can rouse the slumbering teen. Jesus speaks of this extensively in John, chapter 5, where He unites both the themes of judgment and of resurrection:

> JESUS. HIS VOICE REACHES THE DEAD AND WAKES THEM MORE QUICKLY THAN A MOM CAN ROUSE THE SLUMBERING TEEN.

For as the Father raises the dead and gives them life, so also the Son gives life to whom He will. The Father judges no one, but has given all judgment to the Son, that all may honor the Son, just as they honor the Father. Whoever does not honor the Son does not honor the Father who sent Him. Truly, truly, I say to you, whoever hears My word and believes Him who sent Me has eternal life. He does not come into judgment, but has passed from death to life.

Truly, truly, I say to you, an hour is coming, and is now here, when the dead will hear the voice of the Son of God, and those who hear will live. For as the Father has life in Himself, so He has granted the Son also to have life in Himself. And He has given Him authority to execute judgment, because He is the Son of Man. Do not marvel at this, for an hour is coming when all who are in the tombs will hear His voice and come out, those who have done good to the resurrection of life, and those who have done evil to the resurrection of judgment. (John 5:21–29)

THE CHRISTIAN THEN, KNOWING AND BELIEVING IN THE RESURRECTION OF THE DEAD AT CHRIST'S RETURN, LOOKS UPON DEATH AS A TIME WHEN THE BODY SLEEPS, AWAITING THE RESURRECTION, WHILE THE SOUL, OR THE INNER LIFE, LIVES ON WITH CHRIST, REPOSING WITH HIM.

The Christian then, knowing and believing in the resurrection of the dead at Christ's return, looks upon death as a time when the body sleeps, awaiting the resurrection, while the soul, or the inner life, lives on with Christ, reposing with Him. We sing this to each other in many hymns, but perhaps the greatest is this one:

This body in the grave we lay
There to await that solemn day
When God Himself shall bid it rise
To mount triumphant to the skies.

And so to earth we now entrust
What came from dust and turns to dust
And from the dust shall rise that day
In glorious triumph o'er decay.

The soul forever lives with God,
Who freely hath His grace bestowed
And through His Son redeemed it here
From ev'ry sin, from ev'ry fear.

All trials and all griefs are past,
A blessed end has come at last.

Christ's yoke was borne with ready will;
Who dieth thus is living still.

We have no cause to mourn or weep;
Securely shall this body sleep
Till Christ Himself shall death destroy
And raise the blessed dead to joy.

Then let us leave this place of rest
And homeward turn, for they are blest
Who heed God's warning and prepare
Lest death should find them unaware.

So help us, Jesus, ground of faith;
Thou hast redeemed us by Thy death
From endless death and set us free.
We laud and praise and worship Thee.

—*LSB* 759:1–7

I was once told by an elderly parishioner that when he was a young man, this hymn in its entirety was always sung at the graveside after every funeral. I think you can readily see why the old Lutherans valued it so. It teaches us how to think daily about death as slumber, awaiting the resurrection.

The Christian thus rejoices that Christ has made death, the "last enemy to be destroyed" (1 Corinthians 15:26), into something that we need fear no more than our very beds! We have this assurance, though, only through a proper understanding of what will happen at the final judgment.

In Lutheran theology, one of the most often cited passages on judgment is Hebrews 9:27: "It is appointed for man to die once, and after that comes judgment." We remind ourselves of this every morning and every evening when we say our prayers and recite the Creed: "From thence He will come to judge the living and the dead" (Apostles'

Creed, *LSB*, p. 192). That is, when we die, we shall all come before Christ, who will render His verdict upon our lives. Of course, this is confessed not only in the Apostles' Creed, but also in the Nicene and Athanasian Creeds. For example:

> "And He will come again with glory to judge both the living and the dead, whose kingdom will have no end" (Nicene Creed, *LSB*, p. 191).

> "[He] ascended into heaven, and is seated at the right hand of the Father, God Almighty, from whence He will come to judge the living and the dead. At His coming all people will rise again with their bodies and give an account concerning their own deeds. And those who have done good will enter eternal life, and those who have done evil into eternal fire" (Athanasian Creed, *LSB*, p. 320).

The bold assertions of the Creeds are the crystal-clear teaching of the Scriptures. Consider not only the passage cited above from John 5, but also these passages:

> *Peter to Cornelius and his household:* "*And He commanded us to preach to the people and to testify that He is the one appointed by God to be judge of the living and the dead. To Him all the prophets bear witness that everyone who believes in Him receives forgiveness of sins through His name.*" *(Acts 10:42–43)*

> *Paul to the Athenians:* "*The times of ignorance God overlooked, but now He commands all people everywhere to repent, because He has fixed a day on which He will judge*

the world in righteousness by a man whom He has appointed; and of this He has given assurance to all by raising Him from the dead." (Acts 17:30–31)

Paul to the Romans: "For we will all stand before the judgment seat of God; for it is written, 'As I live, says the Lord, every knee shall bow to Me, and every tongue shall confess to God.' So then each of us will give an account of himself to God." (Romans 14:10–12)

Paul to the Corinthians: "For we must all appear before the judgment seat of Christ, so that each one may receive what is due for what he has done in the body, whether good or evil." (2 Corinthians 5:10)

Author of Hebrews: "Therefore let us leave the elementary doctrine of Christ and go on to maturity, not laying again a foundation of repentance from dead works and of faith toward God, and of instructions about washings, the laying on of hands, the resurrection of the dead, and eternal judgment." (Hebrews 6:1–2)

John in Revelation: "And I saw the dead, great and small, standing before the throne, and books were opened. Then another book was opened, which is the book of life. And the dead were judged by what was written in the books, according to what they had done." (Revelation 20:12)

In addition to how the Scriptures reflect the New Testament Christians' clear expectation that Jesus will return to judge the living and the dead, during Holy Week, Jesus Himself extensively and explicitly taught about the impending judgment. The entirety of chapter 25 of Matthew's Gospel deals with the coming judgment in three extended parables: the ten virgins (25:1–13); the talents (25:14–30); and the final judgment (25:31–46). In the first parable, Jesus describes those who are prepared for the Bridegroom's return and who enter into the marriage feast. The door to the feast shuts behind them. The shut door in the parable signals that the age of grace in which we now live has an end, and that we must be prepared for this end.

The parable of the talents stresses the personal accountability that will attend the last judgment. In the parable, the Master returns and settles accounts with His servants, investigating what they did with the gifts entrusted to them. Two were commended and invited to enter the joy of their Master, though they received different rewards based on the extent of their faithfulness. However, the third servant has nothing to show for the time the Master trusted him with His gifts; he hands back what he was given by the Master he regards as hard and cruel. The Master responds in the way the servant characterized him. The conclusion of this parable is stronger than an image of a shut door. Rather, the sentences that conclude this parable serve as a haunting warning: "Cast the worthless servant into the outer darkness. In that place there will be weeping and gnashing of teeth" (Matthew 25:30).

The final story in this chapter unveils the judgment in all its beauty and terror. The Son of Man comes in His glory and all His angels with Him, and He assumes His glorious throne. Before Him are all the nations, and He proceeds to separate people, setting some on His right and some on His left. The ones on the right are declared blessed by the Father and are bidden to come and receive an inheritance prepared for them (note!) from the foundation of the world. Why? Why are they blessed? Because they lived in love: seeing their neighbor in need. The hungry were fed, the thirsty were given drink, the stranger was welcomed, the naked were clothed, the sick and imprisoned were visited. The righteous are shocked! When did we see You, Lord, like that? He answers: "Truly, I say to you, as you did it to one of the least of these My brothers, you did it to Me" (Matthew 25:40). Those on the left are not bidden to come, but to depart. Where to? "Into the eternal fire *prepared for the devil and his angels*" (Matthew 25:41, emphasis added). Note that whereas the Kingdom was prepared for the righteous before the foundation of the world, the fire was not prepared for the cursed humans, but for the demons. Why the dismissal of those on the left? They did not live in love. But they challenge Him. "When did we see You . . . and did not minister to You?" He answers: "Truly, I say to you, as you did not do it to one of the least of these, you did not do it to Me" (25:45). The conclusion to this story is, "And these will go away into eternal punishment, but the righteous into eternal life" (25:46).

How uncomfortable these three parables make us! And well they should. How well have you watched for the Bridegroom? How prepared are you for His delay? What have you done with the countless gifts your God has lavished upon you and for which He will ask an account? Have you seen and served your neighbor in every bodily need or have you excused yourself from bothering? So as Christians we ponder not only our death. We also ponder the account that we will have to give to the One who judges justly at the resurrection; and we may well begin to tremble.

Tremble, yes; but, despair, not at all. Take the last parable in Matthew 25 and think of this: Jesus sees nothing to condemn in those on His right, the sheep; conversely, He sees nothing to commend in those on His left, the goats. How does that fit with your experience? Do you know someone who is completely commendable and good? Or anyone who is completely evil and loveless? I think an honest answer is no. So that parable reflects that it is not just the deeds done in one's life, but how one stands before the King. Those on the right stand in such a way that Jesus sees no flaw, no sin. That, of course, is the work of faith in Him and in His promises. Their faith in Jesus clothes them in His perfect righteousness.

Prior to Jesus' teaching about the final judgment in Matthew 25, Jesus told the parable of the marriage feast earlier in Holy Week (Matthew 22). A king was throwing a great banquet to celebrate the marriage of his son. The invitations went out and were largely unheeded. Those invited were too busy, too preoccupied with the stuff of their lives to stop and feast with the king and enter into his joy. The invitations went out further, to others who were not first invited. Israel's rejection of the Messiah and the invitation being extended to the Gentiles comes to mind with this parable. Things become even more interesting when the king shows up to see the wedding guests. He sees a man there who does not have wedding garments. Most scholars believe that a wedding garment would have been supplied by the king for such an occasion. Thus, this man without the garment shows up in his ratty old street clothes and thinks he is fine just the way he is. He is quickly disabused of the notion! When he is confronted by the king and has no answer for why he does not have a wedding garment, the king commands, "Bind him hand and foot and cast him into the outer darkness. In that place there will be weeping and gnashing of teeth" (Matthew 22:13).

The wedding garment that is pure gift of the Bridegroom to His bride is the *sine qua non*, "something absolutely needed," of the Day of Judgment. The Church tries to hold this before us by the symbolism of the white robe that clothes the newly baptized and the corresponding white pall that covers a coffin. From our Baptism until the day of our death, we must never lay aside the robe of Christ's righteousness which has been given to us and which is ours by the faith He supplies. It is our daily task to remember that our death and the Day of Judgment will come and to cling to what our Lord has given us, in which alone we can appear before Him without sin or stain. To lay our robe of righteousness aside, the forgiveness Jesus wraps us in through God's

Word and the Means of Grace, is to be wholly condemned and cursed at the end; to wear it always is to be found wholly righteous and blessed.

Sometimes I have heard folks complain that Lutheran preaching should focus a lot more on living the "blessed" life. Historically, though, we didn't need to do that because we focused instead on what was infinitely more important: how to die the blessed death. You see, the one who knows how to die the blessed death is the one who truly is set free to live a blessed and joyful life.

> THE ONE WHO KNOWS HOW TO DIE THE BLESSED DEATH IS THE ONE WHO TRULY IS SET FREE TO LIVE A BLESSED AND JOYFUL LIFE.

So how does one prepare to die a blessed death? By daily practicing the putting on of the wedding garment, the righteousness of the Savior. Here is the way that Starck would teach us to do this:

"But if we judged ourselves truly, we would not be judged" says St. Paul (1 Corinthians 11:31). Indeed, if we examine our life of our own accord, charge ourselves with our wrongdoing, and pray for pardon for Christ's sake, God will not judge and condemn us, but He will be gracious to us. For whoever confesses their iniquities and quits them will obtain mercy.

Now the dying, too, should do this. They should reflect that they will have to appear before Christ's judgment seat, for it is appointed that we die once and after that comes the Judgment. Now this takes place immediately after death, when the soul must at once appear before God. If in this world you have been a believer and led a godly life, you will not be condemned; because your sins were forgiven you on earth for the sake of the blood of Jesus Christ, they are no longer remembered in heaven, but remain forgiven. But the ungodly must appear before the divine judgment seat because they died without being reconciled to God. The dying, then, do well to seek reconciliation now, to ask God for forgiveness for the sake of the blood of Christ, and in that way obtain mercy. Thus, the dying are assured that, no matter when and where they die, by a sudden or a slow death, God will graciously receive their souls and will on the Last Day raise their bodies to joy everlasting because they have been justified by the blood of Jesus.

PRAYER

I know, O God, that it is appointed unto men once to die, but after this comes the Judgment. And so I place myself now before Your judgment seat while I am yet living, and wish to be reconciled with You before I die. O righteous God, since I do not know how long it will be before I depart this world, behold, I come before Your judgment and accuse myself. I acknowledge that I am a great sinner. I have transgressed all Your holy commandments, often and knowingly. I have not loved You with my whole heart, with all my soul, with all my strength. I have not always followed in the footsteps of my Jesus. I have not always allowed the Holy Spirit to lead me, as I should have done. I remember that I was made Your child in Holy Baptism, but I have not always lived as Your child. I have often made many promises to You at confession and Communion, but have kept few and have repeatedly been conformed to the world. O Lord, I have not done what is right. The load of my sins weighs me down. I have not walked in the way You appointed for me. My iniquities have gone over my head; as a heavy burden they are too much for me to bear.

O gracious God, You have promised that You have no pleasure in the death of the wicked, but that the wicked turn from his way and live. See, I come now, desiring to make my peace with You, while I am still sound in mind and can recall my past life. Oh, I repent of all my sins. I prostrate myself before Your tribunal and say: Lord God, Father in heaven, have mercy on me! Lord God, Son, the Savior of the world, have mercy on me! Lord God, Holy Spirit, have mercy on me! O Father, I take refuge in Your mercy and confess that I have sinned in Your sight and am no longer worthy to be called Your child. Yet I pray You to be merciful to Your child and not to cast me away because of my transgressions. I flee to You, O Jesus, my advocate! Oh, intercede now for me, a poor sinner, in the hour of my death. For if anyone sins, we have an advocate with the Father, Jesus Christ, the Righteous One. He is the propitiation for the sins of the whole world. Oh, pardon my iniquities for the sake of Your blood, and let me find mercy at the bar of strict justice because of Your holy wounds. Have mercy on me, O God, according to Your loving-kindness. According to Your tender mercies blot out my transgressions. O blessed Holy Spirit, I flee to You! Create in me a clean heart. Bear witness to me that I am a child of God, and that I have received God's favor. Yes, work in me a sincere repentance, a living faith, and a holy resolve to live only to Your glory and to die in childlike obedience to You.

Yes, work in me holy thoughts, devout supplications, and sweet meditations on death. Grant me a refreshing contemplation of heaven and of the future glory. Let my heart hear the comforting words: "My child, be of good cheer; your sins are forgiven you." Then I shall not be afraid to die because I know that the sins that have been forgiven here are forgiven also in heaven. O Holy Trinity, have mercy on me. Let me find grace with You at my departure from this world, and do not charge against me anything I have ever done amiss, but have compassion on me according to your love.

—Starck's Prayer Book, pp. 283–85

The godly habit of thus meditating on our death (considering our death in light of Christ's victory over it, given to us in Baptism) and judgment (rejoicing in the perfect wedding garment in which Christ has clothed us) frees the Christian to live each day in joy. Luther had the hang of this. He once told those who were preparing to die to make sure they had put things in order between God and themselves and had taken care of the disposition of their property, and then they should banish the Spector of death and instead live each moment to the fullest. Once you are prepared to face death as a Christian, you are no longer a slave to fear. As we sing:

My Savior paid the debt I owe
And for my sin was smitten;
Within the Book of Life I know
My name has now been written.
I will not doubt, for I am free,
And Satan cannot threaten me;
There is no condemnation!

May Christ our intercessor be
And through His blood and merit
Read from His book that we are free
With all who life inherit.
Then we shall see Him face to face,
With all His saints in that blest place
Which He has purchased for us.

—*LSB* 508:5–6

Our contemplation of death and judgment is ultimately eclipsed by our certain joy that the One for whom we wait is our Bridegroom. Jesus was at pains to stress this in the first parable in Matthew 25. Thus, as we contemplate daily the "last things," our thinking is not characterized by fear, but rather joy.

The Bridegroom soon will call us,
"Come to the wedding feast."
May slumber not befall us
Nor watchfulness decrease.
May all our lamps be burning
With oil enough and more
That we, with Him returning,
May find an open door!

There shall we see in glory
Our dear Redeemer's face;
The long-awaited story
Of heav'nly joy takes place:
The patriarchs shall meet us,
The prophets' holy band;
Apostles, martyrs greet us
In that celestial land.

There God shall from all evil
Forever make us free,
From sin and from the devil,
From all adversity,
From sickness, pain, and sadness,
From troubles, cares, and fears,
And grant us heav'nly gladness
And wipe away all tears.

In that fair home shall never
Be silent music's voice;
With hearts and lips forever
We shall in God rejoice,
While angel hosts are raising
With saints from great to least
A mighty hymn for praising
The Giver of the feast.

—*LSB* 514

FOR DISCUSSION

1. How does the father in the parable of the prodigal son define "death"?

2. How does this help us understand Genesis 2 and 3?

3. What is the relationship between the death that is cessation of breathing and the death that is exile from home?

4. Describe how our Lord Jesus destroyed death's power over us by "the blessed exchange."

5. How may the Christian face the Day of Judgment with confidence?

6. How does faith in the forgiveness of sins transform an uncertain waiting for judgment to a certain waiting for the advent of our Bridegroom?

CONCLUSION

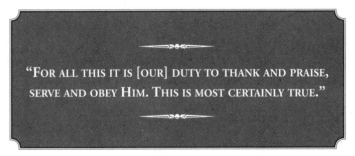

"For all this it is [our] duty to thank and praise, serve and obey Him. This is most certainly true."

So the explanation of the First Article in the Small Catechism wraps up.

It is impossible to miss the tone of joy that rings through these words. This "duty" is not onerous, carrying the weight of law and coercion. It is simply what follows; and what follows is right because our joy and delight are so great. Indeed, this "duty" has itself become part of our joy and delight. It is a fitting response to the greatness of the gifts given; and this joyous duty only grows when we move from the First, to the Second, and then to the Third Article. In all three, the tone of joy is simply unmistakable; and it escalates.

First Article: "He does all this for us so that we may look into His fatherly heart and sense how boundlessly He loves us. That would warm our hearts, setting them aglow with thankfulness toward God and with the will to use all these good things to His praise and glory." (Janzow 70)

Second Article: "The entire Gospel that we preach depends on our thorough grasp of this [second] article. Upon it rests our entire salvation and joy." (Janzow 72)

Third Article: "This is because we see in the Creed how God gives Himself together with all His gifts and powers to us for our help and support in keeping the Ten Commandments—with the Father giving us all created things, Christ giving us all His redemptive work, and the Holy Spirit giving us all His sanctifying gifts." (Janzow 78)

The practical and in-home use of the catechism can give the faithful a whole new way of looking at life itself. It is a way of understanding all of life as gift. When all is gift, we have so much joy and thanksgiving. This "gift orientation" is what both the Large and Small Catechisms seek to form in the hearts and minds of Christian families and individuals.

Lutherans have frequently stressed the disjuncture between nature and grace; but in the catechisms, the unity of nature and grace comes to the fore more than their disunity. Grace discloses that nature is itself a gift of the Blessed Trinity. One can't infer God's grace from nature; but, grace does open up nature as a very good gift that is to be tasted and enjoyed in the way God always intended. Every last bit of nature also points toward the fuller joy yet to come in the New Creation because of grace. When all is undeserved gift—from the Father whose tender love sent His Son to be our Savior and who sent the Spirit to constantly nourish our faith and keep us in relationship with Him—then all our days are filled with countless invitations to enter into the joy of our Lord. It is this joy that gives birth to and fuels Christian piety. We find our hearts singing:

> THE PRACTICAL AND IN-HOME USE OF THE CATECHISM CAN GIVE THE FAITHFUL A WHOLE NEW WAY OF LOOKING AT LIFE ITSELF.

In Thee is gladness
Amid all sadness,
Jesus, sunshine of my heart.
By Thee are given
The gifts of heaven,
Thou the true Redeemer art.
Our souls Thou wakest,
Our bonds Thou breakest;
Who trusts Thee surely
Has built securely;
He stands forever: Alleluia!
Our hearts are pining
To see Thy shining,
Dying or living
To Thee are cleaving;
Naught can us sever: Alleluia!

Since He is ours,
We fear no powers,
Not of earth nor sin nor death.
He sees and blesses
In worst distresses;
He can change them with a breath.
Wherefore the story
Tell of His glory
With hearts and voices;
All heav'n rejoices
In Him forever: Alleluia!
We shout for gladness,
Triumph o'er sadness,
Love Him and praise Him
And still shall raise Him
Glad hymns forever: Alleluia!

—*LSB* 818

It is my hope and prayer that the brief reflections on eight habits of godliness in this book will encourage you to enter more deeply into the great joys of receiving unfailing gifts from our God, the Blessed Trinity. They are a solid foundation that we can stand on because none of these habits center on human achievement; rather, they are all about receiving from God. As we receive His gifts over and over again, a life of piety truly does burrow down, take root, and grow. All to His praise.

BIBLIOGRAPHY

Chemnitz, Martin and Jacob Andreae. *Church Order for Braunschweig-Wolfenbüttel*. Translated and edited by Jacob Corzine et al. Vol. 9 of *Chemnitz's Works*. St. Louis: Concordia Publishing House, 2015.

Concordia: The Lutheran Confessions. Second edition. St. Louis: Concordia Publishing House, 2006.

Janzow, F. Samuel, trans. *Luther's Large Catechism: A Contemporary Translation with Study Questions*. St. Louis: Concordia Publishing House, 1978.

Justin Martyr. *The First Apology of Justin*. Translated by A. Cleveland Coxe. Ante-Nicene Fathers 1. Buffalo: Christian Literature, 1885; reprint, Grand Rapids: Eerdmans, 1975.

Kinnaman, Scot A., ed. *Treasury of Daily Prayer*. St. Louis: Concordia Publishing House, 2008.

Klug, Eugene F. A., ed. *Sermons of Martin Luther: The House Postils*. Vol. III. Translated by Eugene F. A. Klug et al. Grand Rapids: Baker Books, 1996.

Luther, Martin. "Defense and Explanation of All the Articles." In *Luther's Works: Career of the Reformer: II*. Translated by Charles M. Jacobs. Revised by George W. Forell. Vol. 32. Edited by George W. Forell. Philadelphia: Muhlenberg Press, 1958.

———. *The Freedom of a Christian*. In *Luther's Works: Career of the Reformer: I*. Translated by W. A. Lambert. Revised by Harold J. Grimm. Vol. 31. Edited by Harold J. Grimm. Philadelphia: Muhlenberg Press, 1957.

———. *Luther's Small Catechism with Explanation*. St. Louis: Concordia Publishing House, 1986, 1991.

Lutheran Service Book. St. Louis: Concordia Publishing House, 2006.

Plekon, Michael P. and William S. Wiecher, eds. *The Church: Selected Writings of Arthur Carl Piepkorn*. Delhi, NY: American Lutheran Publicity Bureau, 1993.

Starck, Johann Friedrich. *Starck's Prayer Book*. German edition edited by F. Pieper. Translated and edited by W. H. T. Dau. Revised Concordia Edition. Revised by William C. Weedon. St. Louis: Concordia Publishing House, 2009.